A Survivors
ARK

A Survivors
ARK

*From the pits of despair
to the loving arms of Christ*

A Survivor's Story

KEVIN J RYAN

XULON PRESS

Xulon Press
555 Winderley Pl, Suite 225
Maitland, FL 32751
407.339.4217
www.xulonpress.com

Paperback ISBN-13: 978-1-66289-273-8
Ebook ISBN-13: 978-1-66289-274-5

Table of Contents

The Scorch of a Lie

I will not die with lies on my lips
I will not pass without that kiss
I will be satisfied to finally rest.

For if I die with a lie, may darkness
And gloom reclaim me for the abyss.

I will not hide from my fate
I will hold on to love and faith
I will go in peace with his grace.

So make rain fall on my grave
Make certain there's a witness.

I will not die with lies on my lips.

I wrote this book for several reasons. The primary reason is for the purpose of explaining how becoming Christ-centered completely changed my life. Also, I wish to expose many truths as to how and why my mind was completely lost. I was diagnosed with psychosis, clinical depression, anxiety, severe insomnia, PTSD, bipolar disorder, and, not to forget, confusion. I'm a survivor from a lifetime of being devalued, disgraced, deleted with childhood physical, sexual, and psychological abuse.

Furthermore, I share my poetry which, by writing, helps keep me going, filtering my madness, advancing me towards recovery. At times, my poetry was my only glimpse into reality, at the time written. Additionally, I'd like to express how the health care system severely lacks in quality care for mental health patients. If you only have Medicare (as in my case), you can forget about getting psychotherapy. What I received was every combination of psycho-pharmacological medications possible. This kept me over-medicated and no closer to getting to the root cause of my traumas.

Until my self-examination and self-education, I didn't really understand what has happened to me. No one close to me questioned my being over-medicated except my oldest daughter, Christine, who for several years had no contact with me. When she finally did, she voiced her concern of my being over-medicated; eventually, I started to listen and took action, discovering that having a quality Christian-based therapist and/or counselor to guide me has been invaluable. Additionally, group therapy can be educational and cathartic. Having the opportunity and complete freedom to express my deepest feelings and concerns drove me to many truths and self-awareness. Still, to this day, I have to question and constantly check myself to ensure I'm reacting to daily life situations appropriately. This requires constant education and affirmation of some progression. Cognitive behavioral therapy helped immensely.

Always burdening your family and friends with your insecurities is way too much to ask. Often, they are not equipped emotionally or have the wherewithal to handle the task. A quality therapist and support groups are wonderful. My 12-step fellowship is the best thing that has happened to me. This discovery would not have happened without a knowledgeable therapist to guide me. Keeping myself active in a support group such as N.A.M.I. is worth its weight in gold, except when, as in my case, they started saying due to the color of my skin, my emotional difficulties are less than others'. Not able to understand how my trauma is less than others based on the pigmentation of my skin, I had to move away from N.A.M.I.

Doctors always advise diet and exercise as being the key to a healthy life. This is severely understated in the mental health community. I have found that every time depression starts, getting up and walking can be a miraculous cure. I'm still learning how critical a healthy diet is and how much your mood is affected by your diet. In addition, I'm so thankful and feel blessed to have Christine in my life. She is a great dietitian and herbal scientist with copious amounts of detailed knowledge. So, as I said, diet and exercise are somewhat understated while pharmaceuticals are continually pushed. If anyone is serious about wellness at any level in the mental health care system, diet and exercise should be highlighted and given top priority. Pharmaceuticals have a place when in crisis, yet, should be viewed as a temporary help.

After a disastrous childhood, I spent 18 years living with a total narcissist. Not knowing anything about a narcissist until recently, I fell completely in that trap. I was literally driven mad by her actions of devaluing, discrediting, and then eventually discarding me. In all the time I knew her, she never—in her eyes—did anything wrong; therefore, she never apologized for anything, not once. She always, always, played the victim role. Everything that ever went wrong or just didn't meet with her approval was my fault. All concessions in that relationship were given by me. Not once did she ever support me in anything. Looking back, I was insignificant to her, for she never considered my feelings in any situation.

I paid all the bills and did much more than a reasonable share of household chores, but nothing I ever did was good enough. Because I never got any validation or encouragement during my childhood, I completely fall into the narcissistic trap. Since I was already programmed as a worthless individual, for that is all I ever heard, I eventually believed it was just who I was, definitely groomed to be her victim.

In my attempt to be the family provider, I was always focused on being successful and highly career oriented. While achieving success, I was given many opportunities to further that success, but my family life was a disaster. To this day, my youngest daughter views me as a worthless individual, no matter what changes I make to better myself and my situation. She tells me the most egregiously hurtful and offensive things anyone ever said to me. Don't really blame her since she, unfortunately, is completely poisoned by the narcissist who helped push me off that ledge. While there is nothing I can do, I'm still amazed by the situation. One of my biggest difficulties is accepting how we as humans treat one another. I have difficulty watching the news, which is just a daily display of the inhumanity, injustice, and intolerance people show for one another.

A few things I have learned that are for certain are the following:

First, having a kind, loving heart does not mean you will have kind things said or done to you. Unfortunately, that goes for even the people closest to you that you love and trust the most.

Second, finding and having an understanding of spirituality is paramount to finding hope and faith in daily life and any future.

Third, nothing can replace good friends. I've been blessed to have several who still support me to this day. They have been more than helpful fighting the negative influences in my life. I have nothing but love and respect for my friends, I've learned from them to strive to be the type of friend everyone wishes they had. A good friend can help guide you into a higher plane of existence.

Finally, (at least for now), as I stated in one of my poems, (there is no vengeance;there is no revenge). Although there are never apologies admitting their crimes, no matter what we do to one another, we must find forgiveness. Forgiveness, I've found, is a key to help quiet the mind and cleanse the soul.

This book is my way to say to all those that gave to me any support over the years, I am grateful and thankful. Your kindness was not wasted on me, not one iota.

Thank you all!

My Life

This life, my life,
Is like a drop of rain
Clinging to a blade of grass.
The grass bends from the weight of my burdens.

I fear losing my grip at last.
Will I be swallowed by the earth?
Or will the light of His Son lift me
Beyond the shadows of my past?

This life, my life, is like
A drop of rain clinging
To a blade of grass.

Dedication

I'd like to dedicate this book to the following:

Most of all my daughter, **Christine Elaine Ryan MS R.D.N.** Your love, support, and encouragement help me in more ways than I could ever comprehend.

My friends and few family members:

Dr. Jeffery Haugh, your friendship and spiritual guidance is invaluable and will last forever. Thanks.

Michael and Shabnab Curtis, always there with open hearts and home. Great advice and guidance. Mike is a true brother who understands precisely what that position entails.

Steven and Deila Case. Steve is the closest one that truly understands the pain endured; he understands how physical pain is nothing when compared to mental anguish.

Rocky Walker, our trips to the temple did more for me than I can ever say.

John Dixon, such a spiritual giant who returned and endured every call made - loved our conversations!

Ronald Gilbert always got me to church; during that time, we discovered how much we have in common.

Jeffery Link, a great listener and good friend who is gracious and always reliable.

Kevin Mooney, you tried your best to help put me back together when I first fell apart. I couldn't answer your questions then, but after all these years, I now can. I only wish it didn't take so long.

Frances Crist, always there giving to others and a great friend; please stay healthy.

Maggie Warner, my constant reminder that God is great and ever present; Maggie is never judging and always respectful.

Debbie Holden, you gave me hope with encouragement to continue writing; I loved our time together. I will always hope and pray the very best for you.

Bruce and Kathy Ryan, your help was invaluable, such a blessing to me.

Michael Ryan and Betty Beyer, you guys got me out of that studio apartment, helping me focus on brighter days. It would be a waste if I didn't take what you gave and not succeed.

Thank you all for your love, support, and compassion. I would have never been able to persevere without any one of you.

A Survivor's Ark—Dramatically True

By the hand of God, with His strength,
I have been guided unfailingly throughout my life.
Such trust and love, never before, was realized by me.
Here, now, I proclaim, shout, testify with a clear
Mind a newly purified heart, I stand upright
With a pride only given by our Savior, through
endless blessings and gifts, my abilities grow.
Having something here to say quantifies His many gifts.

As a child, I felt so cursed,
At conception, it must have been
Violent from the very first.
Never to dream or have a trusting relative
To provide the slightest bit of love.
My life began as dragons ripped my flesh,
Ungodly parents and siblings did to me,
The most unfathomable, worst abuse,
On my frail body in my moments of innocent youth.

As a boy, so tortured I was,
Nights filled with terror were routine,
Paralyzed with suffocation that muted my screams,
Hands of that dark entity pulling me down—
This was not a dream. I tried to claw and grapple my way back.
Unable to move, finally today I know now, it was
Christ that always reached down, lifting me up.

As a man, confused by those demons and beasts,
I carried great burdens of weight, on my back falling
And tumbling about. Quickly left behind that unholy house,
With nothing to smile or laugh about.

Holding in all my pain, I joined the Navy,
After which I raised two beautiful girls.
Maintained and provided for my family, all the while
Being undermined by a self-involved, unloving wife.
She isolated me as I isolated the child inside me.

So many times, I stumbled, tripping becoming drunk,
Drugged, and lustful, piling on hatred, shame, and guilt,
All this upon myself. Receiving no encouragement,
Not even one word.

My mind was reeling in pain as every expression
Of doubt spewed out negativity, shame in violent
Drunken rants, and fits of rage. So overcome by
The disease of doubt with perceptions of failed expectations
Not understanding or knowing promises that the
Savior has made, I felt oh so lost,
As my wife used, then deleted me.

So many attempts of suicide out of depression
From being filled with fear, self-recrimination,
Blame, feeling I've failed again and again.
In my lapse of reasoning and inward discrimination,
So certain of nothing, yes; then I lost my mind.

A vision or intense dream came to me, it shattered
My very being, a fear over all fears, fell on me. With
Such clarity, for if I do not follow a righteous path,
The future was more than bleak, it was all laid out.
To become nothing more than a wasted piece of wood.
To float in a void of nothingness for eternity.
Separated from my Creator. Thought I would just be forgotten by
The universe and God.

And there, His hand always on my shoulder, guiding me
To the Scriptures, I then devoured looking for the answers
I sought, why and of what purpose, if any, was my mandate?
Could no longer accept that endless misery, therefore;

The Dhammapada, King James Bible, Book of Mormon,
And Pearl of Great Price became my daily reading. Those
days filled me with a new understanding of hope.
Yet still cautious, not yet holding or having true faith.
I had found a new hunger!

It is the word of God! Knowledge and understanding
Were not enough.
Realizing God was guiding me through my many
Challenges into right solutions with clear answers,
Giving me endless signs. Out of confusion into new
Light and greater understanding stood before me.
Demanding choice and action.

So, hear this; from a man that bled too much, Jesus took my
Hand, gave me such a powerful hug,
Feeling now that always I have His love, reformed and a softened heart.
Started speaking compassionately, only by His strength.

I built a new benevolent foundation, untying all my
Hatred I kept in nautical knots, binding new, a truce,
With all my devotion and praise, I give to God.
Now I turn to face my Savior, my God, never again
Will tackle any challenge on my own, for powerless,
I know now without Him. Most certainly
I am (now in the refiner's fire).

Never again, I pledge, will I ever deny our Lord and Savior,
My God!

Winters Solstice

Abide these winter days,
As lines of an April birth remain.
Out on a frozen pond, alone, a
Skater framed,
Silent are these days,
A solstice celebration that born,
Christmas day,
For the Christ child, we praise.
Though no gifts will be exchanged,
Yet, in a memory, kindness does remain.
It warms to the bone.
As bitter wind cuts through a solemn skater's cheek.
A rush of angel wings, sung this day to sleep.
As "God Rest Ye Merry Gentlemen" plays,
It carries across the valley with joy for this day.
Friends to hold and keep,
Are gifts He gave.
A heart is always moving toward the one that calls,
Shepherding all His sheep.
A prayer to you this day, be mindful of His gifts.
Spread joy as you travel so far away from me
All that I'll ask, for a lone skater on this pond,
bring back, a song so tender, joyful and sweet
For me to hold and sing to sleep.

—The Lone Skater

The Pugilist

A million old soldiers have faded away,
While a dream lives on forever.
These old eyes will never lose,
When there is strength in something to say.
Collecting logical verbs for obscure views,
In my stance against the abusive.
This pugilistic poet stays complete in verse,
To twist back the turns they made.
Those aerial boundaries mock gravity's grip,
As fisticuffs clinch that final verdict.
Forever steadfast in stance remains,

—Your Pugilistic Poet

As we go from God's gift of strength to strength, we can gain at great length insight into His plan. So, stay straight in place and follow with grace that path back into His hands.

CHAPTER 1

Number Nine

B orn on September 14, 1954, in Toms River, New Jersey. There was nothing particularly special about this date except, for me, the curse that clouded my lonesome soul. It is certain to me (based on my treatment) that I was not conceived or born out of anything known as love. This date will not go down in history or ever be a day even celebrated, inasmuch as it never was. Born that day, I was the ninth child of what would eventually be eleven children for Herold and Ester Ryan. As the ninth child born in the ninth month, in 54, which equals nine, I will, at least in this lifetime, forever be number nine. My name, Kevin James, seems just something they picked out of the air; I guess maybe they thought it sounded good? Never was I told anything about it, so there are no ties to any family lineage, etc.

This was and is a highly dysfunctional family. No love, religion, or encouragement to survive of any kind was ever shown, just constant ridicule and verbal, sexual, and psychological abuse. My given name didn't matter, for I was always identified as the "long eyelash little sissy," the "cry baby," and eventually by one of my brothers as "quickie the queer". So, I was never called by my name but always something condescending and derogatory.

We didn't stayed in New Jersey much longer after I was born. Having no recollection of that place, there is really nothing I can say about New Jersey. The only thing my mother talked about my first year is that they gave me penicillin and I almost died. I don't know why I needed an antibiotic, but being told I'm allergic was the only thing of any value she ever said to me. For that matter, I was never spoken to as a person by either of my parents. If acknowledged, it was always in some demands, such as "Sit down," "Shut up," or "Get out"—never anything welcoming.

The earliest thing I can remember is at the house in Baltimore. We lived in O'Donnell Heights on Elliott Street. That place was a government-subsidized housing community. With a relatively small housing for so many children, none of us had a bed to ourselves until much later in life. Being the youngest boy, many years younger than the next brother, proved to be difficult in every way.

One of my earliest memories is when my father wasn't working. My two younger sisters were still in their cribs, they were both crying. My father was yelling at me, (I was about four or five at the time) telling me to keep the babies quiet. I was trembling and begging them to stop crying. I felt so lost as to what I could do. My father came in and threw me to the side, yelling that I was a worthless piece of shit.

It wasn't long after that when I witnessed my parents fighting. They fought often back then. I seemed to me my father was drinking rather heavily at that time. There was always fear throughout the house when my father was home. Often, it was announced he was on his way home or coming down the street, everyone would scatter. Eventually, the police were called and he was taken off to jail. When he was away—perhaps still in jail? — my mother had a relationship with a cab driver. I remember coming home from kindergarten, which was only a half day at the time. I arrived home around noon and my mother was in bed with him. Those types of visuals stay with you for a lifetime. I was told to get outside, which was normal protocol - send the kids outside, always the standard answer for everything. Children should be seen and never heard is one of the many gems you could hear them say.

They left me alone with my brothers and sisters very often. I can't think of any other memories of my mother in those days. My oldest sister, Judy, claimed that she is the one who raised me. I don't remember much of her, either. The only thing I remember is that once I tripped and fell on a broken bottle, seriously cutting open my hand. A neighbor took us to the hospital and I got several stitches.

When it was time to get the stitches out, my sister Judy dragged me to the hospital. I can remember the difficulty I had keeping up with her pace as we walked to City Hospital. In the hospital, I once had to take a leak, but Judy wouldn't listen to my pleas. I tried and tried to pull away from her, but she wouldn't listen, since she was busy talking to her friends. I ended up wetting myself, she finally took me to the restroom. Very abruptly, she demonstrated how upset she was with me. She turned my shorts around, perhaps thinking it would look better if I was just wet in the back. Don't know, but I do know she considered me to be a huge burden and nothing more.

Always being sent outside was a pleasure to me, for it always seemed much safer out there. Once I was playing in the dirt under a tree in the yard. My father called me inside and lifted me up to a mirror in the living room. He proceeded to announce what a little disgrace I was, saying I was a filthy little burden, he wanted nothing to do with me. He threw me down, kicked me, and demanded I get out of his sight and get cleaned up.

My closest brother in age was several years older and had nothing to do with me, unless it was for him to push me around or to satisfy him sexually. I vividly remember him on my back; after gratifying himself, he got up, went into the bathroom, and left me there crying. I was so confused; I didn't know what to do or what to say and truly, there was nowhere to turn. Had to just take it for what it was and just how things were. It didn't stop there. He once put me under a blanket with my sister. We were naked, and he told us to get in a sexual position. I remember when just five, having no idea what was going on or what a sex position was, I took the lead from my sister and complied with his wishes.

One of my other brothers walked in on us but didn't say a word. He looked around and saw my brother hiding behind the door naked. He just shrugged it off, turned, and walked away. It was my brother who showed me how to manipulate myself and masturbate. He often forced himself on me, and all I felt was guilt and shame as far back as that. This caused me to start chronically masturbating, quickly becoming a daily routine. Once in the first grade, I did it while in class. Looking back, my teacher must have seen this; yet, she didn't say anything.

Shortly after that day, that teacher had a meeting with my mother. My mother had her over for lunch. I don't know what was discussed, but the result was more confusion and pain. When my father came home, he started yelling. "I'll have no freaks in my house." He was yelling at me, I didn't know what was going on. So confused, not understanding what was happening; therefore, I could only cry as he sent me away. I had to get out of his sight, for he kept hollering how he couldn't stand to look at me.

The sexual abuse didn't stop for several years. A friend of my father's took me with him one day. I had just turned six the month before, he took me to see *Spartacus*. We ended up at his apartment in his bed. Think I fell asleep during the movie. He had his way with me and was playing with me when his supposed nephew came in. He was very upset at what that man was doing with me. They argued, I was shocked, afraid, and confused. Dreaded fear and shame rushed over me and never left. Nothing was ever said about that day, don't think I ever saw him around again. The guilt and shame so heavily embedded in me still remain. Later on, when in middle school, one of my brothers was staying at the house. He came in one night after a date. I don't know whether he had been drinking or not, but he forced himself on me. He took plastic from the dry cleaning in the closet and wrapped his penis with it. He forced it in my mouth and kept shoving it in. I just remember choking and silently crying. He just held my head and kept shoving it in. After a few minutes, he took off the plastic, so he could finish. So ashamed and hurt, I felt nothing but hate for him. I'm still trying to deal with the resentment. He always treated me with disgust and continues to ridicule me. Certainly, it was violent; it was rape. There is no other way to look at it. I carry that stain and the guilt and shame and he continues to look down on me.

Shame

Shame is a security bit,
Embedded inside the ID.
It pulses to apply
Conscious morality to
The ego that helps guide
The choices made
In an often-confused mind.
Now it identifies me,
For I know the pain of shame.
Every lie that they tell,
I take the blame.
With permission granted only from above,
Those I try and try to love,
It allows me to press on.
I feel only the immense agony of shame,
Should I pray or just cry out?
Through dark, still nights with muted screams,
Can I beg for the end of everything?
Should I try each day and lift my head?
Or remain in fear of the unknown and dread?
Can I find the sister known as guilt?
Should I accept responsibilities without
The act of actually committing any crime?
Or take on all those strangers' dreams,
Hold or grasp that light,
That long fell out of my sight,
In a glimmer of others' might.
Forever, this shame must last.
For it has long revealed its task,
Just, to what end, I have to ask?
Are my mind's security enabled
And built determined to outlast
The past that will not pass?

The Ark

From the deceptions of fake realities
To the fortress of fruit-bearing trees
Among the antithesis of antiquities
In the slums and ghettos of the city
To a ramshackle frame on the muddy.

Poverty never did escape me,
The richness of Christ now guides me.
All His love is laid out before me,
He has always been here with me.
I love how He decided to teach me.

Now a peaceful serenity,
Now at rest after each day,
Now at the altar of new beginnings,
Now with a purposeful sway,
Now a life worthy of living.

Finally, I feel a righteous desire just to be.

Whatever social skills I was developing happened while playing with my sisters. After all, they were closest to me in age. Because of this, I was tagged the little sissy. I don't understand why this was my fault; I was always ridiculed for it. I was never called anything much other than "long eyelash little sissy" in those days, a punching bag for everyone, including my older sister closest in age to me.

This sister that was a year older would often beat me up. My father was always so pleased with this. After all, I was just a little sissy. He would put boxing gloves on us and make us fight in the front yard. This went on until one day, I had enough and let her have it, hopefully putting an end to her punching on me. The reaction from my father was to beat me for hitting a girl. The only message I got was, things were hopeless and nothing was to be gained by me.

We were so poor that once, when I was in grade school, I found a silver dollar in the gutter. I was excited when I got home and announced to everyone, "Look what I found." Immediately, it was snatched away from me, I was accused of having stolen it. Where and who from didn't matter; it didn't belong to me, even though I truly found it. It was taken away, we were able to have hot dogs for dinner. Meat was something we didn't get very often. Dinner usually consisted of butter macaroni and beans or some type of lama bean or navy bean soup. The fact that I was accused of being a thief didn't bother anyone except me. Everything I ever got a little excited about was ripped away and replaced with some hurtful, cutting remark.

I often survived on sandwiches from a woman down the street, Mrs. Waters. She always called me Calvin, which I liked; she was nice to me and was special. Also, I would walk to McDonald's and clean their parking lot for a hamburger, fries, and shake. Additionally, I would go to the cleaners and pick up lunch for the workers there, and they would give me a meager tip. No one at home was ever looking for me; I was pretty much on my own from the very beginning.

Now, I've come to realize that the hatred and abuse came part and parcel for being the runt of that litter. Being the youngest boy with four older brothers and six sisters was complete torture. Once, my brothers hung me out the second story window by my feet. They teased and threatened to drop me. When I showed fear and cried out, I was the little sissy. Another time, they put me in a metal closet, filled it with cigar smoke, and proceeded to throw in lit firecrackers. However, it was the time they took a knife to my penis and threatened to cut it off that really disturbed me. I had nightmares for the longest time after that. In fact, I had night terrors and nightmares throughout my childhood well into adulthood. To this day, I still fight having night terrors. Thing is, I really don't remember having dreams, at least nothing like I read about or see in movies.

I'm just a joke to my siblings, the crybaby, the sissy, the worthless piece of garbage. Not one of them has anything to do with me; they all ignore me, as though I'm not good enough or worth a minute of their time. Once I thought, maybe they felt guilty, but the fact is they never consider or think about me. That gets more obvious as the years pass on.

My mother once told me that I walked like a stripper. I didn't know at that time what a stripper was but knew for certain that it wasn't good. So, I tried not to move much when walking. If I found myself relaxing and forgetting, my father would give me a good swift kick in the ass, as he called it. I do know this much: if I was born with any amount of homosexuality in me (as some doctors claimed), it was most certainly beaten out. They forced my soul, the very essence of my being, into many back-alley proclivities. So, I've got to say this: to put a label on it, was I, in fact, born gay? I will never know, since my natural development into sexuality was robbed from me. That is what I do know, as a fact; my entire development such as socialization and any sense of self-actualization was taken from me. I had absolutely no sense of self-worth and until I found my way to my 12-step fellowship, Christ, the path of righteousness, I was empty, truly in a void of nothingness.

The Runt

The runt of the litter suckled hind tit.
Acquiring a taste for bitterness,
The runt of that litter was exiled from the pack,
Acquiring a taste for loneliness,
And alone he wanders off;
So now, it's rain, dirty valleys,
Rat-infested alleys.
That's all there is,
That's all there ever was!

CHAPTER 2

The Acquired Taste of Bitterness

When, amazingly, I reached the age of nine, we moved in the dead of night out of O'Donnell Heights. We ended up in a roach-infested dump in Hamden, Baltimore, on Chestnut Avenue. This place was horrific; we could never keep the roaches down. Our next-door neighbors, I often remember, said that the roaches didn't eat much, so why bother with them? The ironic thing was, there was a home exterminating company just two doors down.

It was a three-story house with a small heater on the first floor. This was supposed to heat the entire place. Well, it, in fact, didn't do much of anything. Even on the second floor, you were cold. By the time you started up to the third floor, you could see your breath. In the winter, you were always cold. And in the summer, the heat was sweltering.

In the neighborhood, I had to quickly develop self-preservation survival skills. Going to and from home to school was always an adventure. I can't remember a day that didn't require me to fight somebody. Being a small-framed, skinny boy, I must have looked like an easy prey. But I was strictly instructed by my father and brother that if I ever lost a fight, don't come home, for they would beat me even more. I didn't really want to hurt anyone, yet I most certainly did. Every block was territorial; once, I threw a rock at a boy that didn't belong on my block. He was quickly riding away on his bike and I hit him on the head with that rock. He fell down off his bike. I was amazed I could throw a rock that far and accurately. I never saw that kid again. However, I never forgot that image or lost the guilt of what I had done.

A few of the other neighbor kids would often play stick ball in the alley. One part of that alley had so much broken glass, you couldn't see anything but broken bottles. Anyway, the stick we used for stick ball was what my father used to put against our back door to lock it. So, when one of the other kids threw it up on a garage roof, I had to climb up after it. There was a fence around the home exterminating company parking lot. This you could climb up to get on top of the garage. However, it was greased up to try and discourage us from climbing it. Still, I had to get that damn stick; I felt my father would have certainly killed me if I didn't. The result that day was I fell off the roof and landed on my head. I ended up being taken away in an ambulance. I woke up several days later in my bed after being in shock. Furthermore, I only remember waking alone and the blood on my pillow. Not one person made any attempt to comfort me through this or ever with any struggle that I went through. Since I missed so much school that year, I had to repeat the fifth grade.

It was about when I was ten or eleven years old that my father took me camping. He was purchasing a piece of property in Keys, Fairy Acres, West Virginia. We were there clearing out the underbrush. He had a tent set up and a cooler with some food. Our dog, a German shepherd named Butch, was with us. My father left me and that dog in those woods, explaining only that he'd be back in a few days. He had given me a shovel and told me to dig a hole for a latrine. He took off, I can only guess this was done to toughen me up, since I was, as he always said, a worthless little sissy. But the joke was on him. In reality, I felt completely safe in those woods. felt much safer than I did at home. Those woods were no match for the streets of Baltimore.

Taught myself how to swim that summer in the Shenandoah River. It was only me and Butch, the dog. Butch almost drowned me, as he was trying to get me to, I guess, save him. Looking back, there was no one around at that time and if I were drowning, no one was there to help. My self-preservation skills had to kick in then. I learned early no one was ever there for me. I was always alone, my siblings would prove to be my kryptonite. Looking back, I was a fool to ever worry or consider what they thought or felt. Not one of them ever spoke to me as a person, let alone one that had any value.

We moved to Norwood Heights, which was west Baltimore and a little nicer neighborhood. It wasn't much, just a nicer house, no roaches this time. I had to go to junior high at Rock Glen. I was a white minority student there. Had to fight every day just to stay alive. For some reason, the Black girls were nice to me; they would often keep some of the boys from beating on me. Every class was disrupted; the other kids were all so unruly. Never learned much of anything there, for it was just impossible. Did my parents care? Not at all; my sister who was a year older dropped out. She couldn't take it. She ran off with an FBI agent that lived across the street from us. He had a wife and several children, but they ran off to live together in Virginia. Yet, I was the one that was always told, wouldn't amount to anything. Around that time, my mother slapped me across the face, screaming I was worthless. You have to understand the impact that had. My mother never said much of anything and never did anything to protect me from my father or my siblings. For her to actually take a position, any position, it had to be pure hatred. I was bringing home good report cards, but she didn't even look at them, just doubled down on the hatred my father kept spewing out.

There was one glimpse of kindness out of my father. One Christmas, he bought me a small, cheap plastic record player. It really wasn't much except a great escape for me. I started collecting music then and never stopped (music reading and writing are still my escape). That small act of kindness from my father came with a price from my mother. She pulled me aside and with disdain in her voice explained that my father got me "the damn record player." If she had her way, she would never have bought me a thing. There was so much hate in her voice; I'll never understand.

She really didn't need to tell me that. I already knew, for never once was my birthday celebrated, even after watching that the others' were. Think that may have sporadic with others; at least, they had a chance. We were extremely poor in my younger years; still, she did at least make an attempt to celebrate with others. A few times, she explained that they didn't have the money when my birthday came around. After a while, she didn't even try to explain. Thinking back, she could have used some of the money she had been taking from me since I was thirteen.

Truth

Found truth can be in a snowflake.
That falls gently finding an eyelash, causing you to blink.
In glory, truth covers you like a warm blanket.
It shrouds you and holds all your dignity.

From a midnight streetlamp to the first breath of morning light,
Each utterance gives a gift,
To clearly see the wisdom of a sage.

Truth will comfort and protect you from the narrowest of paths through
The darkest of times, until the end of your days.

When I went to high school, I traveled across town on the east side to Patterson High. It wasn't much better than the west side, except I was no longer in the minority. Between working and taking the bus across town every day, I didn't have much time for anything else. Tried out for the swim team and made varsity when I first jumped in the pool. That was a shock to my system. My coach, was so excited watching me swim, I couldn't believe it. No one in my entire life was ever interested or excited about anything I had ever done. That was so totally new to me, having someone actually say something positive about me. I couldn't believe it and could never accept it as being true. Even though the team was undefeated that year and I won several meets, I was doomed to fail. Failure was ingrained in me, for I was beaten down by everyone in my family.

The next year, my father didn't allow me to stay on the swim team. Even though I held three jobs (Baltimore Candy and Tobacco Company, Gino's, and the Chesapeake Ranch Club on the weekends), he considered me lazy and worthless. By wanting to join the swim team, he said I was just trying to get out of my chores at home. Oh, yes, that was my other job: cooking and cleaning for "the house," which was never ending.

The fact is, when my sister ran off with the man across the street, she left behind a car and my parents with the payments. I took over the payments and paid the insurance. Once I was working late at Gino's and on my way home when a group of punks, greasers, hoodlums, whatever you'd like to call them, began following me across town. They caught up with me downtown, stopping in front of my car, and prevented me from moving forward. They got out and started beating on my car. Then they smashed in the driver side window. They pulled me out of the car and began beating me. I managed to get back in the driver's seat and put the car in reverse to get around them. I made my way to the nearest police station and filed a report. Not only that, but I never heard from the police again. When I finally arrived home, my father hit me across the side of my face, yelling it was my own damn fault. He hit me so hard I fell to the ground, my ears ringing so loud I could hardly hear him yelling at me to get up. He kept kicking me, saying, "You must have done something to provoke them." After all, everything was my own damn fault since I was still breathing. My crime was that I was still alive and burdening my parents. That was just another opportunity for him to demonstrate his hatred for me.

Yes, my father was always so full of hate. He would sit there getting drunk, watching TV, reading the paper, and yelling about how the "blacks and Jews are destroying this country." He and my mother both smoked, the air would choke me. When I didn't stay and watch TV, I was the weird little bastard that would never amount to anything. I heard this crap from them over and over again, never ever getting an encouraging word from either of them. In fact, when my father got drunk, he would look for and find a reason to beat on me. He loved kicking me and would so often chase after me. Until one day, I had enough; that was it. He was chasing me up the stairs. Running to my room, I stopped at the top of the stairs, turned, and told him to kill me right then and there. For nothing, I said, could he ever do or say that would ever change what my opinion was about him. At that moment, I was finished. I remember the look on his face. I was reminded of a short story I had read, "Thus I Refute Beezly." The look was as though the giant winged beast from the story had ripped him from the steps; there was not much left but a morsel of a man. He never hit me again, but he still made his negative comments and showed his disappointment in everything about me. For me, the victory was empty and disappointing, for we never had any type of healthy relationship, never had a conversation.

Don't Beat Your Chest

Don't beat your chest so proudly,
Not in front of me.
You shouldn't be so proud,
Teaching a child to hate.
With that clinched raised fist,
You should have laid a deadly blow.
For this black sheep has some pride.
Proud of that day, he stood up.
So don't beat your chest so proudly.
Not in front of me.
You shouldn't be so proud,
For this black sheep is still afraid.
Afraid of that you, inside of me.
Don't beat your chest so proudly,
Not in front of me!

lways since, thirteen and had a paper route and every a job since, I gave my mother the money. She told me she would keep it for me and give it back when I needed it. When that day came, she acted as though she didn't know what I was talking about. She never gave me a penny back or anything, ever. What a kick in the ass that was. Additionally, when I went into the Navy, I had to leave my car behind. My father sold it, never giving me a penny. His answer was that I should have never left it at his house. Yet, my oldest brother left a car (a Shelby), my father kept that for him for several years, when he was in the service. Obviously, I wasn't worthy of any consideration from either of my parents. After all, I was a disgrace as far as they were concerned. So many times, I was sent away from the dinner table. My father would be yelling, saying how much he couldn't stand to even look at me. My mother would just sit there and say nothing, just with a disgusted look on her face.

Mother never intervened, never stood up for me. She was cold and distant, treating me with disgust. When she wasn't being cold, she was just hateful. So many times, she told me I wouldn't amount to anything. Not once did she ever show any type of affection toward me. Never did she speak to me as a person, always giving me the feeling that I wasn't worth a minute of her time.

When I graduated from high school (something I was always told would never happen), the graduation was held at the Civic Center in Baltimore. I got a ride there with my parents. However, they left me and I had to take a bus home. They didn't tell me they went to their favorite bar, the Golden Globe. It didn't matter that much because I was so depressed, realizing soon I would be kicked out of the house. Depressed because I had nowhere to go. I didn't know what to do. Even though I was working three jobs, I wasn't making enough to get my own apartment.

In my teenage years, I spent most of my time (when not working) alone in my room, since I was told so many times what a freak I was, and they had absolutely no use for me. It was only a few days until I'd be kicked out. Having no chance for college and nowhere to go, I was depressed. Bought a bottle of Boons Farm wine and drank it in my dark room. I was depressed and full of anger all the time. The only choice I could see was to join the Navy. Even though the draft was ending that next day, I signed up for the Navy. I chose the Navy because no one else in the family had been there. Plus, my brother Mike, who was severely wounded in Vietnam, made me promise I would never join the Marines.

When I signed up, I received a deferment date for after the summer. Foolishly, thought I would have the summer and get my private pilot's license. However, I failed my first shot at the written test. Also, my father made things so difficult, I had to leave right away.

CHAPTER 3

The Navy

Well, there I was, forced into a situation due to not having any direction. My understanding was that I had no other choice. So, I started that summer in boot camp at Great Lakes. It was a welcomed relief and a huge culture shock. Many of the other guys in our division actually missed their families. This I didn't understand; I had never felt so safe in my life. We had a guy commit suicide, also the guy in the lower bunk under me had to be released and sent back home because he missed his mother so much that he went berserk one day. What was all this I was experiencing? Some people out there that actually cared about their family? More to my point, they had family that cared about them. Wow, what a shock.

In boot camp, I had the same problems as in school when showering with the others. I felt extreme guilt and shame in the showers, doing everything I could not to stare at anyone. But I had that same sex attraction forced upon me by my brothers. It was all so difficult, but I kept it hidden, which I did very well. One day, when on my first carrier call out at sea, I was raped by someone I trusted as a friend. I still have night terrors over that. This is something I never could mention to anyone. I felt it was somehow my fault. Became even more isolated, never talking about my time in the Navy. Until recently, I was not able to speak about it, for the shame and guilt were just too much. So, I kept that part of me hidden and buried it deep inside. Also,

I kept the other abuses I had suffered, never telling anyone the truth about my dysfunctional family. While many spoke of the joys of family, I could only think of the thousands of sorrows I had to keep hidden.

Did very well in the Navy; boot camp was a breeze. only got into trouble once when accused of talking in ranks. The senior chief tried his best to break me, but he couldn't get through. He was no match for what my father had put me through. He sent me to something they called happy hour. It was punishment, we were drilled by a Marine sergeant. It was forced calisthenics while having to hold onto our rifle. For being a little sissy all my life, this was certainly easy. When we returned to our company, the other guys were crying and complaining. I just took it all in stride, for it really didn't have much effect on me. The petty officer kept trying his best to get to me, but he didn't have a chance of getting through the walls I had put up.

Although, promised a slot as a jet engine mechanic, I was sent out in the fleet. They said I would get to go to school later on, but this never happened. I wanted to get as far away from my family as possible. Therefore, I chose the West Coast, stationed aboard the USS *Enterprise* (CVAN-65). At the time of my arrival, it was in dry dock at Bremerton, Washington. Truly, it was a marvel to see such a huge ship. I felt so insignificant and small beside it.

Loved it in Bremerton, A few shipmates got an apartment in town and lived together there. It was a constant party. Not ever having any moral compass, I was then introduced to drugs and alcohol. Thought I already had some knowledge of these things but, in reality, I didn't know a thing. Having no filter and not much will to live, everything was in excess.

Once we went out to sea, the party stopped; we were put to work seriously. It was time to straighten up, and that is just what we did. Worked in the catapult division as an aviation boatswain's mate. I got myself trained and checked out in as many stations as I could. Soon, became the center deck operator. My job was to calculate the amount of steam required to launch the plans. It was a quick calculation based on the weight of the plan and knots of the ship. I liked that job until, one day, I had to stop a launch due to not having enough steam. Anyway, that didn't go over well with the deck officer. He attacked me afterward down below deck. The senior chief witnessed it and asked if I wanted to press charges, didn't see the need. So, as it turned out, I was offered the job of divisional yeoman. took that in a second; what a nice job.

We were stationed in Alameda, California and spent several months at sea each time we went out. We went to Vietnam during the evacuation and saw quite a bit of equipment being destroyed and dumped overboard. With all the commotion over the war, I really wasn't political. Spent my time trying just to maintain some control over myself. When in port, we would always party like there was no tomorrow. We had copious amounts of pot and alcohol and, of course, there were always women. Eventually, I couldn't smoke much pot; it just seemed to make me stupid and paranoid. So, I stuck mainly with beer, but when you drink a lot of beer, you are still drinking a lot.

Once, when out on liberty, a few friends and I were in Berkeley Hills and got busted for pot. We ended up in the Oakland Jail. The three of us were the only white faces in that place. It was a large room with beds laid throughout. Everyone was just standing around acting tough. A rather large black man tried to get my friend Jerry to make his bed. Not willing to put up with anything from anyone, I stepped in. Telling Jerry that if he made that bed, I'd kick his ass. Everyone just walked away from us. At that point in my life (even though I was small), I would stand up to anyone. After all, I had stood up against my father, so I could do anything. When they handed out lunch in jail, I was the last in line. When it got to me, there were no trays left. They were all already handed out. Looked around and saw a guy with two trays in front of him. Sat down next to him and took one away from him, just daring him to do something about it. Carrying so much anger, I was ready for anything. No one in jail was willing to fight me. All I knew was anger and never thought about where it came from.

Barriers

Breaking the barriers of your sound waves,
The surrounding angles are all so strange,
A mentor of madness or wise old sage.

Raw courage with everlasting refrain,
Coldness served up with a twist of a name,
Plied with her sex for a month and a day.

Only having blues, a wish you tried to proclaim,
Knowledge of the right with shallow pities and parses,
Walking in silence, now they're walking away.

Breaking the barriers of your sound waves,
Stemming from sadness, glad to give way,
A clinching claw for stopping air waves.

You're sniveling sneak you whimpering brave,
Standing in defeat, of that dark driven beast,
That's a mountain of hope that stands in your way.

You torturous burden, you'll never be saved,
Now you're putting birthday candles on a fresh grave.
So, you try breaking the barriers of these sound waves.

My Breath

Pressed my cheek against the window,
Feeling the cold just outside.

My breath entangled the despair and humiliation
Which fogged the screams
From my site,
Drawing lines across the pain
With stick figures that walked on by.

Sounds of silence fed imaginations
Of a brighter light.

A yellow moon sits in the night's
Dark blue sky,
As I faltered and forgot every hopeful lifeline.

W as about to get married to Susan, my high school sweetheart. Had some money on me to buy the ring. Also was supposed to make my way back East for a visit. Needed to use most of the money to bail myself out of jail. My friends had to stay back in jail; they were let out early the next week. We went to court and my supposed "friends" got a lawyer and testified against me. So much for friendship! I took my chief petty officer with me to court as a character witness. Luckily, the judge felt the case was a waste of his time. He admonished the arresting officer and threw the case out. I learned that friendship meant nothing and everyone would turn against me, if given the chance.

Back on the ship, had to deal with the guys that tried to testify against me. They tried to tell me how it wasn't their fault, blaming the lawyers. Anyway, I stood my ground and as with every situation, my response was to fight. At that time, I didn't know any other way to deal with things. If I wasn't fighting, I was burying my past down deep with alcohol and drugs. I was always doing everything in excess, there was not much that mattered to me. The possibility of marrying my girlfriend was the only positive thing I had to hold onto. So that's just what I looked forward to.

My time in the Navy taught me many things. Found out that I really wasn't stupid or even lazy, even though I couldn't spell or even properly structure a sentence. Some people actually listened to me, responding to what I had to say. All the alcohol and drugs were my way of keeping the demons at bay, stifling the most recent abuse imposed on me. Becoming the divisional yeoman helped me immensely. Taught myself how to type and organize my days. Got along with the officers in that office very well and even became friends with a few. When at shore, I would play requite ball with the lieutenant commander. This was against the rules, but it didn't seem to matter to anyone. As long as I was able to keep my past in the past, things went along very well. Even considered for a while that I might stay in the Navy. At least there I was making advancements and had some people that respected me.

I ended up getting married; it seemed at the time the right path to take. From the very beginning of that marriage, Susan wanted me out of the Navy. She moved out to Alameda, California with me and we rented a studio apartment. It wasn't much, but we seemed to be happy, something I had never experienced before. This all ended when Susan said she was diagnosed with cervical cancer by a Navy doctor. This all turned out not to be true; it was Susan's way to manipulate the situation and get me out of the Navy. She acted so distraught, she stopped using birth control, eventually becoming pregnant, and then it was the constant worry she would lose it. That didn't happen; still, I was released from the Navy a few months early on due to hardship. I wasn't happy about leaving the Navy, but Susan convinced me that I was.

Iron City on the Sea

Gray skies, cold salt air, kept your lungs clean
Strait of Juan de Fuca,
One hundred miles of rocks that meet the northern sea.
Lummi Indians were there first,
Salmon, oysters, clams, that's what they ate.
Dark pacific waters were oh, so inviting.
So tranquil to be swallowed by that sea.
That youthful sailor knew early of its invitation.
That ship is an iron city on the pacific sea.
He became a veteran of some foreign war, with not one political thought.
Only the war within himself as he became,
A part of that war machine.

Cat walks, open hatches, all did lead to
Bulkheads of that distinguishable teal green.
Illiterate letters were written home and given
Up for his sibling's ridicule.

A youthful sailor, but yet older than the old man of the sea.
So soured by the hard gifts his short life had given.
That toothpick of a boy, washed his arms in gasoline,
keeping him hard and mean
That crazy lightweight, spat in the face
Of all those that got in his way.
That sea placed pressure on those knots
Within him.

The nip of each knot, never let hate slip away.
That tough faced streetwise punk, few
Would ever go toe to toe, as he
Scrapped, boxed with shipmates for
Drawing their blood set him free.

A killer in his soul, with a skull cap on his skinhead
Sweating in those steam voids no
Other man could ever get a grip on
That wiry skinny boy who was taught
At such an early age, never lose a fight
Or else there would be hell to pay
Today it's hell he pays each and every day.

Chapter 4

Married with Children

As I previously mentioned, I married my high school sweetheart, Susan. We had dated throughout my time at Patterson High. There were a few other girls, but Susan was the one that I felt actually listened to me. At least, that's what I felt at the time. We spoke on the phone just about every evening and on weekends when I wasn't working. She never asked for much when we dated; she said she didn't want to spend my money, which I worked so hard for. Everything about her felt right for me. Her parents were nice to me; they seemed to be a good family. They were definitely not like any family I had ever known.

Susan was and will always be the only woman I ever truly loved. She was the first person I had ever met that showed, what I thought was, a genuine concern for my well-being, that person I thought I knew will always hold a place in my heart. Unfortunately for me, as it turned out, the love I had for her was unrequited. She had her own agenda; I was just her vehicle to get away from her family.

A Kiss

Our breath entangled and it
Knotted itself in our passions' heat.
We spent ourselves together, and we
Drifted off to sleep.

There were distant melodic chords,
A tango to the oneness of our dreams
In perfection's slumber, we did retreat.
Melding our hearts as one, in frozen
Moments of eternity that we volunteered.

Neither her nor I could move or speak,
As we did fit so entirely, deep in that loveliness.
Out on that ocean boat, we were pampered by soft waves in a lullaby.
It brought on madness from our kiss.

Out there afloat, and there adrift, if
we were never to wake from the sea of dreams,
It would forever and ever been,
From that kiss.

S usan, as I said, was my one true love. She changed my life completely, thinking I was better off with her. Until she entered my
life, I had no idea what love was, since I had never experienced any
closeness toward anyone ever before. This was my opportunity to
start my own family and treat them the way I had always felt individuals should be treated. I had a chance to break those chains of abuse,
a chance to focus on something positive for a change. Anyway, this
was, in fact, the start of a new life for me as well as for her, since I felt
we were in it together.

We were married while I was still in the Navy. I made it back from
the West Coast on a thirty-day pass. The wedding was in a Lutheran
church that neither one of us belonged to. Still, I don't understand
why we had it in a church. Neither one of us came from a religious
background. The reception was held in a small hall over a volunteer
fire department. The guests consisted mainly of her family and very
few of mine. We had a small buffet, which I think just consisted of
cold cuts and salads. There was absolutely nothing remarkable about
it. The one thing I do remember is my father got in an argument with
her mother. My attention was focused only on how quickly we could
get out of there and start our honeymoon.

After the honeymoon, we moved into a small studio apartment in
Alameda, California. It was small but very nice; it received a lot of sun,
so it was very bright. Susan got a job at a local yacht club, typesetting
their paper. I was still stationed on the *Enterprise* and doing very well
and considering staying in the Navy. Then, Susan announced a doctor
had told her that she had cervical cancer. As she explained, she would
not be able to have children. As I said, since she acted so distraught,
I applied for a hardship release from the Navy. They reassigned me
to the base and I worked as a carpenter and then a bus driver. We
stopped using birth control, and just as quickly, she was pregnant. This

was our miracle child, and she was conceived out of complete love; at least that is how I felt.

At that time in my life, I had completely dissociated myself from the past. It was as though nothing bad had ever happened. If not for the occasional nightmare and night terrors, I would have completely forgotten my childhood. Still, I carried a lot of anger around, which would only come out when I was drinking. In those early years, I didn't drink much because it always reminded me of my father. Never wanted to be like him in any way. Also, when it came to sex, I kept that completely separate from love. To me, one had nothing to do with the other-- and it still doesn't.

I was discharged from the Navy, we moved back East; Susan was very insistent about that. My feeling was there was nothing back there for me, but she was having our first child and wanted to be with her family. I had no prospects when we got there. I don't know why I did this, I took a job at my parents' restaurant. It was a small liquor and luncheonette in Baltimore. This was not at all what I wanted to do, but the fact is, there was a child on its way. I didn't work there long; as with everything, they made it unbearable. Basically, they didn't want to pay me and their plan was for Susan to work at their house as housekeeper and me at the luncheonette without pay, so they just wanted a couple of slaves and that was not about to happen!

Quickly, I got a real job with Quarry Supplies in Baltimore. Before I knew it, I was the assistant manager, handling every aspect of the operation. Susan and I, along with our miracle girl (Christine), moved into a small apartment on Mary Avenue in Baltimore. We were happy then; at least I was. Worked very hard at that job and enjoyed it. My manager was Clay. He once told me that he hired me since I was so persistent. Guess that's because I was so desperate to get away from my parents. Got along very well with Clay. He taught me quite a lot about the practical aspects of running a business. Never being satisfied with my position, I was always looking out for new opportunities. Soon, one came along: my sister Kathy helped me get a job at

Morrison Knudsen at a consortium in Columbia, Maryland. This was a great opportunity. I was hired as an expediter for a project called M.A.S.A.C. Found out then that I was an excellent negotiator. They put a lot of trust in me and made me a field expediter, began traveling extensively. This was exciting at first; however, just as quickly, it became drudgery. I developed an excellent reputation and the management trusted me. When traveling, I always amused myself by visiting a local museum, finding a local restaurant, and/or in the evening, going to the best place in town. I acted like I was some food critic or something; anyway, it was entertaining. On the planes, bars, and in restaurants, I'd always listen to strangers' conversations. having fun making up my own conclusion of their stories.

After the M.A.S.A.C. project ended, Morrison Knudsen offered me a position to move with them to another project in South San Francisco. Susan was pregnant with our second child (Erin) at that time. Being so busy trying to advance my career, I didn't realize Susan was having a relationship with Pete. She met him at the company where she was working, Agnihotra. That place turned out to be a cult. He (Pete) was supposed to be an artist, yet I never saw anything artistic out of that guy. She convinced me nothing was going on between them. They were just friends that liked getting high together. So, I felt moving to California would be a good thing in many ways, especially since that relationship would have to end.

We moved out to San Mateo, renting a $250,000 handyman special. That was a lot of money back then, but it was a nice house. There were fruit trees in the yard and it was in a good neighborhood. Susan, as I said, was pregnant with our second child and followed me out. I was utterly surprised and devastated, in fact, when she showed up with my daughter Christine and Pete tagging along. What the hell was that all about? I should have realized then that the marriage was over. But the old saying that love is blind has a lot of merit. What a fool I was; you see, my disassociating sex from love was really working against me then.

Susan didn't stay out West very long. After having our second child, Erin, she just couldn't wait to get out of there. She took the kids for what was supposed to be a visit back East for Christmas, never having the intention to come back. She called and told me if I wanted to see the kids again, I'd have to move back East. Eventually and foolishly, I quit my job, even though it was a great job with a great future. Ended up having to move a house full of furniture and a car trailing behind the moving van. I did this completely by myself. I don't know how I did it; still I did, within four days.

Admittedly, I couldn't have done all that work and heavy lifting without the help of cocaine. Couldn't afford it, but I had a friend from the Navy, Danny, who gave it to me. He lived in San Jose and was a dealer of some kind. But anyway, he would give me an eight-ball whenever he dropped by. As I said, couldn't afford it, so really couldn't make it a habit. When I was alone in San Mateo, I was somewhat pro-miscuous for a short duration. Depression set in, didn't really care much about anything. The shame and guilt from being addicted to lust was working on me. The drugs kept me from doing anything about it. When drinking, all my inhibitions went away and the anger took over. I tried my best not to drink. However, I did spend some time with a guy I worked with and his girlfriend, but that only lasted a week or two. I never did have a love relationship with anyone else but Susan.

When I finally ended up back East, moved with the promise of a job with Doorman International. When I got out East, the job was no longer available. So, I was stuck and had to live with Susan's parents for a short while. That was absolutely horrible; I had never felt so uncomfortable. Her mother would smile in your face and then back-stab you as you turned the corner. Once, she pulled me aside and admonished me for not looking hard enough for a job, telling me I had to get out there and go door to door until I had one. Couldn't convince her that the type of job I needed, required a solid resume, appoint-ments needed to be set up, and so forth. She was so unbearable that it was a completely miserable time for me. Neither her nor her daughter

Susan took any responsibility for the position we were in. The fact is, if Susan had supported me with my job at Morrison Knudsen, there wouldn't have been a problem.

Eventually, a job did open up with Doorman, we moved into a split-level house in Sykesville, Maryland. Somehow, that bastard Pete was still hanging around. Susan swears they were just friends. Once, while attending night school, I came home late to find the two of them engaged on the living room floor. He got up, and I punched him in the face; he gave little response, only saying that he thought I understood. What crap that was; my girls were asleep right down the hall, they're out in the living room, having sex. I should have divorced her then and there. However, my guilt and shame of my past kicked in again, telling myself I wasn't much better. In fact, looking back, actually I was, since I never loved anyone else but Susan. Certainly, it wasn't fair having my nose rubbed in it daily.

Why I put up with that for so long is beyond me. How cruel she was to do what she did. I tried and tried to forgive her, but the trust was completely gone. Still, she made no effort whatsoever to end that relationship. She even had an abortion, not ever discussing it with me. Had no right to inject my opinion, as she put it. Pete took her to have it done; she confided in him, not me. It was possibly his anyway. Still, the way she rejected me then was a lot to take. She worshiped him as though he were some kind of saint; it was sickening to watch.

I buried myself in my work, always taking on highly stressful positions, which I excelled in. She kept that bastard around and used my feelings of inadequacy against me. With all my success in business and the great strides I had made, my personal relationship was absolute crap, never wanted to admit just what she was doing to me. The psychological torture was, at times, the hardest thing I had ever endured. How could this woman I loved so much treat me with such disrespect and disgrace?

We moved into a hundred-year-old farmhouse in Smallwood, Maryland. That wasn't my choice, either; when we were looking for a house, she brought Pete along. I wanted a place we looked at in Mount Airy, but we ended up getting what she and Pete wanted. Even though we just missed out on the hippy years, that's all Susan wanted to be. Looking back, it was deplorable the way she treated me, not to mention the effect it had to have had on our children. She invited him to live with us, using the excuse that he had a bad heart and couldn't live alone. Why should I have cared about that? He treated my oldest daughter, Christine, terribly, while Susan stood by and just let it happen. Once, he was accusing her of eating his cereal, she was sobbing. I had to intervene; what a bastard he was. What a stupid thing to accuse a child of. My position was she could eat anything she wanted and if he didn't like it, he could leave.

As with every situation, when I got a glimpse of clarity and voiced it, Susan would turn it against me. Somehow, I was always considered the bully. Between night school, my job, and working on that house and property, I had no time to even breathe. Yet, one day, she turned and said that she thought I had another life outside the family, which really, I did: with work, school, and my lust defect, I was truly isolated. Even keeping that under control as best I could, it still came out once in a while.

She was always with Pete, getting high and whatever else they were doing. When she finally left and divorced me, I was shocked, after all I had done for her over the years, paying all the bills, taking care of the house, putting up with Pete, etc. She said as an excuse when leaving that she didn't feel she was enough for me. Maybe she wasn't, never even trying to work anything out, simply isolating me, which based on my past, fell right into her narcissistic trap, even though she had that long-term relationship with Pete. Still, I never loved anyone else but, as always, she managed to turn everything around on me.

She left at a time I was suffering with extreme depression and was suicidal. I was drinking a lot then, and the guilt and shame were stronger than ever. My father passed away in 1991. This had a lasting effect on me. The day he passed, I was at his bedside and he was just fit to be tied. He was as angry as I had ever seen him. He turned and looked at me one last time and told me I was nothing but a pain in the ass and that's all I ever was. Even though I left the hospital directly after that, I felt it the moment he died. On my way home, had to pull over to the side of the road because I knew it was at that minute he died. felt it so strongly that I started to cry a little. What a complete loss I felt, for he never got to know anything about me and I never knew him. This was just another thing I had to keep inside. I did plant a tree in his honor and even though he never showed me any kindness, I felt a loss.

When I had first started going to counseling, the therapist requested I bring Susan along. She absolutely refused to go and left me on my own, just when I needed help the most. Our marriage vows meant nothing to her; looking back, she never supported me in anything. Every argument we ever had, she would turn it back on me, bringing up something that may have happened 10+ years earlier. Even though totally out of context, logic never mattered. She was always right about everything, never apologizing for a thing. With my background, I was an expert at dissociating. Blaming myself for everything was the common theme. She just used me all those years, always getting her way. I ended up alone in that house, spending the nights in the dark, drinking bourbon, all I wanted was to die.

Today, each memory of her mars my brain, leaving scars that cut deep, branching out like crooked fingers pointing to a sea of misery.

That Rose

I strangled that rose
Until its thorns dug deep,
Causing me to bleed.

I captured all its beauty
As the aromatic scent invoked
Magical memories.

Then each pedal quickly withered
Falling from love's decay.

Tears of rage flowed as
Blood did rise around my feet.

There I stood ankle deep,
Wading in the regret of mystics
She kept secretly.

Never will I hold another
Rose of such beauty,
For nothing remains except the
Tether of this dying rhapsody.

Painted Bird

He once painted a bird
In a multitude of colors,
Like a child's kaleidoscope
It's now seven shades of gray.

A canvas of disgrace
Complete with muted screams of agony.
That bird once painted gold and green.

A plume of pride has been lost,
He continued to attempt to paint.
Unimaginable, was once its beauty.

He painted that bird to perfection
Then he
Slashed open his face.

Petals of a Daisy

Once, silos in your eyes stood tall,
Now you speak of dust and that's all.
Those crumbling, decaying silos house only blackbirds.

I'll talk today of how together,
We used to chop all that wood.
For once with me, you engendered
Such love.

Now you Creak every time you speak,
Sitting in that chair I made from
Branches of old willow.

Those bare feet every season
Took its toll.

As all those diamonds turn to rust,
I wonder whatever happened to that
Daisy, I thought I knew so well?

CHAPTER 5

The Unraveling

Doorman International was the only job I had ever been fired from. Even though it was a blessing to finally be rid of that place, I took it pretty hard. Working as the manager of the materials department included the warehouse and shipping and receiving. This was a small operation and the work was extremely stressful. My manager was a thief named Charles. Everyone in the industry knew how difficult he was to work with. There were so many questionable business practices, it was hard to keep up. A job would be quoted at one price with the required grade of material and then, if won, everything would be replaced with downgraded material. Anyway, when I was asked to forge some documents and refused, he let me go. What a bastard that man was. In the long run, I made out much better, keeping a bit of my integrity intact.

After Doorman, I landed a job with Bendix. Bendix was quickly bought out by Allied, which, just as quickly, became Allied Signal. Started out as an expediter and advanced to a buyer position in no time. This position was extremely stressful and high pace. Never seemed able to keep up, but nonetheless, I was one of the best in that position. Being a very hard-nosed negotiator, my reputation in the industry was well known. By traveling all over and extensively, I became well versed in the manufacturing processes. This helped me in countless ways to reduce the overall product cost. You can definitely say I was very successful in that position. Today, I'm viewing success in a much different light, after I spent over eighteen years there and developed many business acquaintances.

Once Honeywell took over Allied Signal, everything quickly changed. We were told, if we held a position for more than five years, we were stagnant, and they had no use for us. Everyone had to reapply for whatever position they held. We were all fired and rehired by Honeywell. So many initiatives were introduced to streamline the processes, it was difficult to keep up. The majority of our time was spent on team building and process improvements. The actual work of maintaining proper documentation of procurement suffered. Passing audits became forensic work. Building documentation after the fact made that job even more difficult. Team building was outright dog-eat-dog practices as to who could get notice and advance their career the furthest. Holding on the best I could, became the team leader for what was called COE (center of excellence). We were tasked with the job of outsourcing what we once did ourselves. This was even more high paced and stressful than anything I had ever done.

Taking this new philosophy to heart, I took what I knew and moved over to a position with a supplier, Pioneer Standard, where I started out as a product specialist. I didn't want anything to do with that operation or Allied. However, due to my knowledge and expertise, they kept dragging me back in. Eventually, I became East Coast regional manager for Pioneer's Kitting and Turn Key operation.

With my personal life in total disarray and the stress of my job, the panic attacks began. I had no idea what was happening, and I thought it was a heart attack. When they first started, when on my way to work, I had to pull off to the side of the road. When the doctor told me they couldn't find anything physically wrong, I returned to business as usual. Nothing was the same and my home life was in total chaos.

When Susan left, I was even more suicidal. My drinking was getting even worse. My first attempt at suicide was to hang myself in the barn. Fortunately, this failed since the beam I tied the rope on broke. I ended up on the floor of the barn, rope around my neck and a bruised back side from hitting the ground. After getting myself together, I sobered up and went back to work. The work at Pioneer was extremely stressful and busy. The people at Allied Signal (Honeywell) were getting more abusive and totally unreasonable. On top of my stressful job and personal life being a mess, my dog, Butch, was killed one morning crossing the road in front of my house. I loved that dog and his death had a considerable effect on me.

At this time, I went off the deep end. I cashed out my 401(k) and bought a Volvo C70. I started back to using cocaine, out every evening, just going insane. Went driving down US 70 at 120 miles per hour late one evening, just totally out of control, crazy. Began dating again and doing everything I could to keep the business at Pioneer going. It was a total roller coaster ride every day.

The depression would not leave me alone. If I didn't pass out from drinking every evening, the night terrors would certainly take over. Before I knew what was happening, the suicide ideation kicked back in. This time I had a gun and was ready to shoot myself. My neighbor from across the street called the police. I had spoken to him earlier and whatever I said concerned him. When the police showed up, I was up in my bedroom with the gun to my head. The only thing I remember is the cop telling me that since I only had a 22, it would not likely do the trick. He told me that the 22 would probably only scramble my brain, and I'd become more of a burden to my family.

Being delirious at the time, they took me away, ended up in the hospital. They put me in a small padded room, but they forgot to lock it. Next thing I knew, I was walking down route 32 toward my home. That police showed up again, they locked me in that room securely this time.

954

Past thinking of
Night terrors that did last much too long.
Held on a ledge with bleeding fingertips.
My grip, a mountain it could have split.
But I marched out of that oculus
Filled with sadness, through a wake of tears.

There was a room with padded walls, in which
More than a week was spent. Focused only on these wrists.
Counting every hair, watched as they danced.

A light in my head, perhaps His glory, so effective,
more than a monk, more than a priest.
His words, a bond that each day and still is.

Some questions cannot be asked
As He did return, ever endured call.
It was then I felt His greatness,
Which will never diminish.

As I drown in the tears
Of the eye of that Fallen Angel,
The one that fell on his bloody battled sword,
I sing a sad sailor's song
A thousand miles from the ocean,
Captured in my heart is a meditative spirit,
A recluse of a soulful beginning
With enticements of a fantasy
Driven here to lose again, as
Heaven falls all over me,
I look to see the face
Of one mightily forgiven,
As the wind takes my spiritual
Unforgettable weaknesses away
I shudder as I think.

Slap Feet Hard

The first few seconds wake
Slap feet hard against the floor,
How did you find sleep?
Did you have any lucid dreams?

Now look over that bed that someone else had made.
Did those many demons come to call?
Slap feet hard against the floor,
It's socks, then underwear.

For in that hell, the floor was cold.
Take just a few seconds to reflect.
Just how did sleep find you?
Did that terror require your defeat?
Just what was that paralyzing suffocation
In the stillness of night?

Now slap those feet hard, realize you're still alive.
So, swallow any remaining pride,
And slap feet hard to face yet another demanding day.

S pent several weeks in that hospital. Diagnosed as bipolar with PTSD and clinical depression. They just put me on medication and I had to participate in group therapy, learning about triggers and safety measures one should always take. I really didn't get much out of that visit; I only learned that I couldn't drink. Also, it was strongly suggested I start psychotherapy, which I did. They didn't want to let me out until I had someone on the outside to sponsor me. Not having any family around anymore, I could only think of my friend, Rick. Always traveling, Rick couldn't help, and he suggested another friend, Kevin.

Rick picked me up at the hospital and took me home. When we got there, he poured all the alcohol I had down the drain. To this day, I never again touched a drop of alcohol. I never even had a desire to touch that stuff. I know it just brings out the anger and makes me mean. Not only that, but I can't even try to defend my actions when drinking. So, taking the advice of doctors, started attending therapy sessions. However, in so many ways, the group therapy made everything worse for me.

I was still extremely depressed and suicidal, but I allowed the group of individuals in therapy into my life. Yet, another huge mistake—I just didn't care anymore. The people I met in the hospital were from Baltimore. As it turned out, they had no desire to get sober and were only concerned with getting high. They introduced me to crack cocaine, and I became even more of a mess. I found out then that some of those in the hospital were there only for free meals and a place to sleep for a few days. I ended up supporting a couple for a short while, going along with everything they wanted to do. Felt nothing mattered, since I wouldn't be alive much longer anyway. The medications didn't seem to have much effect on me.

Eventually, got myself back together by getting rid of those individuals. Went back to concentrating on work, but work was getting harder and harder each day. The operations I ran began losing profitability and Allied was squeezing it dry. It was my responsibility to present a proposal to management outlining how and why it should be shut down. After having put so much of myself in that business, it was difficult laying everyone off. There were a lot of good, hardworking individuals; I had looked in their eyes and now had to lay them off. This was probably one of the most difficult things I've ever done, but for the business, it was necessary. Management offered me a position in Cleveland. I attempted this for a short time, but I just didn't fit in there. They don't like people from Baltimore in Cleveland; that quickly became clear to me. So, I ended up back in Maryland. I attempted my hand at sales, but I'm not and never will be a salesman. That takes a different breed of man and wasn't for me.

I bounced around for a while and attempted some odd jobs, but nothing was sticking. I ended up renting an apartment from my friend, Mike, in east Baltimore. Got a job at a manufacturer in Woodlawn. That was a step-down from where I had been. Having to start over, I was excited to get back into some routine. At that place, I was able to utilize a lot of the process improvement methods I learned in the past. Not only was I the senior buyer, but I ran the storeroom and shipping/receiving department. Being a small company, we all wore several hats.

It was at this time when I met Brad and Grantly. When I was first hired, my supervisor informed me the management was very religious and I should keep my distance. Being myself, I didn't listen and treated them just like anyone else. After some time, we became pretty good friends. Was writing some poetry then and would share it with Grantly. When reciting "Interpret This!" to Grantly, he told me I should see a psychiatrist. After explaining that I already was, we started talking about the spiritual aspect of life. That poem I shared was written directly after having a very intense dream. My interpretation was from the Dhammapada, which I read many years earlier. I believe it explains that if one doesn't follow a path of religiousness, then you become nothing more than a wasted piece of wood.

Interpret This!

A lucid intense dream
Paralyzed by the sight
A burning screaming bleeding piece of wood
Once well planned small growing larger, closer
Feeling the heat,
Hearing that high-pitched scream,
Smelling that burning blood.

Multidimensional grains,
That took years and years to grow.
Vivid colors, deep with texture it was.

That burning screaming bleeding piece of wood.
Floated out in midair,
With nothingness all around.

So, the long journey coming back from what was, at that time, my biggest fall seemed to be coming to an end.

Images

Tears from a crow
Have rusted out the belfry,
Dew from the moor,
Have made those steps slippery,
Fog from the lake,
Has stopped the sun from shining.

Every breath you take,
Whispers out your insanity.
Trees sing with joy,
Songs that sound so strange.

Now winding down to a roar,
Friendly familiar grieving.
Those stony mountain rocks,
Bleed each soul they take.

There's confusion on ahead,
When wishing for belief.

CHAPTER 6

LDS/The Church

When Grantly offered to send missionaries over my house, I was intrigued. My poem "Interpret This!" really got me thinking about my own spirituality. Writing every day at the time, I was open to try and find some answers. With all I had already been through, the journey was going to be difficult. But I agreed because I was more than ready to get started on a new chapter in my life. Grantly gave me a Book of Mormon and I devoured it within a few weeks. It gave me so many things to think about, questions just started piling up. By the time the missionaries came over, I was ready to argue my case against whatever they had to say.

The missionaries stopped by on a Saturday. They had prepared some lessons and I listened for a while. However, once I started my questions, they weren't prepared with all the answers. I felt, well, that's the end of that. Didn't expect to hear from them again, thinking they were like the Jehovah's Witnesses that stopped by once. Never heard from them again either. Anyway, the next Saturday, there they were at my door, armed with answers to my questions. That just wasn't good enough. I had to come up with even more questions. So, my journey with the church began adding some clarity in my life.

Clarity

Psychosomatic induction,
Metaphysically accepted,
With sublimation of moralities.
Spiritually gifted,
Yet stereotypically not.

Steadily, specifically thinking of God.
Confidently speaking,
Religiously thinking,
Broadening my horizon with clarity of thoughts.

Contemplating this contemplation,
Now clearing a new path,
For the brightest day is still to come.

To His Calling

For I am pleased to His calling
From a path of dark and dreary days
I found my way into His light,
The path of blissful eternity
I stumbled over ancient stones
Falling into welcome pews, now,
For I am pleased to His calling
In this place I face true religious dogma
Where I found truth in spirit
Scripturally sound, which brought me
Around to God above.

Today my spirit rides higher at His feet
My days count greater, void of misery,
For I am pleased to His calling
Greater than that ancient speech
Greater than that dark and dreary
Greater than that beast
I found myself in the Light of Christ
For I am pleased for His calling me.

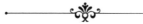

After several weeks of going back and forth with the missionaries, I agreed to be baptized. Before this could happen, I had to change some basic things. I gave up coffee (a little difficult), tea, and alcohol— well, I didn't drink anyway. The real difficult item was those damn cigarettes, that dirty habit I picked up in one of my hospital stays, believe it or not. In order to go outside for a break from the ward, you needed to smoke. Someone offered me a pack and I took it just to get out for a few minutes. I was never really committed to them anyway. But it was harder to quit than I expected.

Last Cigarette

These windows bleed the heat of afternoon
A promise was made,
If the lighter does not light,
For this last cigarette, there will be no need.

An unwilling first strike was made.
Thin walls revealed a neighbor's routine.
A teenage girl, today again she screams.
It's a matter of generations times three.

As I drag across thin, moist lips,
Ingest poison from this last cigarette.
A fan above circulates,
The emptiness of this room.

Somewhere, happiness there must be.
Not for that girl or the grandmother she beats.
Not for this one that fills his lungs,
With smoke of a last cigarette.
Above all this neighborhood noise,
There is a silence not to be ignored.

As those cops bang down their door,
These walls can stand a new coat of paint.
This afternoon, bleak dog day demands to be heard.
This fallen man remained unimpressed,
As a last cigarette now sworn against.

Everyday people can never comprehend,
The last cigarette's greatest sacrifice.

I started attending church regularly. I spent a lot of time with the missionaries. Work was going very well. I enjoyed my conversations with Grantly. I began to respect everything about Brad and Grantly. These guys were genuinely good people that demonstrated love, respect, and concern for one another. This was all so foreign to me, but it was something I was missing and desperately wanted. Grantly has a large family and treats each of his children with unconditional love and respect. That was so refreshing to see. In fact, traveling with the missionaries, I met with many families. In each home we visited, it amazed me to witness the love they showed each other.

Grantly was the bishop of the Towson Ward then. Unfortunately, due to my address, I was in the Chesapeake Ward. This didn't really matter much because the people in the Chesapeake Ward were just as friendly. I was quickly assigned a teacher position and took my assignment seriously. Getting prepared for each week's lesson allowed me to learn as much as I could every day. I took my baptism promises seriously, especially the law of chastity. I had come to accept daily masturbation as a normal way of life, until a bishop from the church explained how that wasn't the case and that I should practice the law of chastity. This worked out OK for me, and out of respect for the garments, I always kept myself clean. Finally, it seemed I found a home, a place that fit; it was just what I needed. Things were looking up, so what could go wrong?

A Cog

Burning bridges, starting a new life.
Rejoicing each day with personal peace,
Sent here to fight armed with will.
Battle bruised, now it's welcome in homes.

By listening to an articulate heart,
The man that was is all but gone.
It's now open hearts and open homes.
God has softened this man of stone.

Found this path in the eyes of a friend.
Climbed this day a few new rungs.
Never noticed before, the sky is blue.
The truth of mystic is answered in old ways.
A cog in His overall scheme I found myself to be.

Forbidding foreboding, such weight He lifted.
My friend brought that spirit along.

Together we three restored an old dead heart.
Every ounce of praise due to One.

Joyous pride, raised up having fought for one.

With everything going well, I still began getting depressed. I started smoking again, not much, just cheating now and then. Night terrors started back, I was hearing voices again. The voices were always of men and women outside my window. They were always talking about how worthless I was, telling me I should just kill myself and do everyone a favor. I did the best I could to ignore those voices and sought out professional help. I had to get back on medication, which always took its toll on me. I hid this the best I could from those at church and work, and I just kept going. In the Scriptures, I was reading the Old Testament, specifically Leviticus. I found that to be a laborious task. Anyway (and I'm paraphrasing), there's a part in Leviticus that tells us not to lash out at our parents. If you do, will you be damned? As in the Ten Commandments, honor the mother and father. Obviously not the exact words; that's what I got out of it. This bothered me so much, I had to stop and consider my parents and how I was treated. How in this lifetime could I ever come to love and respect them? Maybe God will, but I won't; that's the difference between God and me. That sounds like a Lyle Lovett song, yet at that time, it was true for me.

Leviticus

Oh, Leviticus! you have so depressed me.
Born of such nakedness, shame is on me.
Died a thousand deaths still you demand,
That last drop of blood of me.

Say I should fear a face unworthy I'll never see.
You speak of judgments, punishments, with no sanctuary for me.
Not a child of Israel, a violent God, is He?
They broke commandments on my back,
so I broke those chains that held me back.

Oh, Leviticus! you have so depressed me.
You demand tithes to redeem, of this, I simply cannot conceive.
As Job had so much more
Then God ever gave to me.

A just and perfect man, never blessed could I be.
Those gifts and that petition for a pardon of transgression,
Not worthy of the breath I take each day.
Oh, Leviticus! You have so depressed me.

My sacrifices of Thanksgiving are at my own will.
Still have nothing but a broken man,
With illegitimate prayers.
Oh, Leviticus! You have so depressed me.

There I was, once again fighting those demons. I found myself one evening literally boxing the shadows in my apartment. It all seemed so real; having hallucinations wasn't something new. Those days, that was reality was for me; I couldn't tell the difference. Somehow, I needed another change, but just didn't know what to do. So, I made another wrong move, taking a job in Sterling, Virginia.

This move was a big mistake. Running from problems that are in your head doesn't make much sense. Having no one that took any real personal interest in me, all my mistakes I completely owned. There was nothing about the move to Sterling that was good for anybody—not that company, not me; it was just bad all over.

I lived in Lansdowne, Virginia, in a nice apartment, but my mind was somewhere else. I attended the church in Sterling but wasn't accepted there at all. I attempted to get the bishop to give me a calling, but he threw me out of his office and never spoke to me again. I'm not even certain what happened; I just remember I needed to stay active. That rejection set me back several years. Work didn't go well either; I had a lot of confusion. I ended up back in the hospital. I had a large knife in the hospital lobby, threatening to kill anyone around me as well as myself. After some time in that hospital, I went back to work, but they fired me the same day I returned. They didn't even give me a chance to try and explain. I wasn't really surprised, since I was certainly unstable.

I started back seeing a doctor a few days a week and going to therapy. The new medication always seemed to work for a little while. Inevitably, they all stopped working after some time. I was so tired of taking that stuff, but I didn't have much choice because the confusion would always come back.

My friend, Mike, got me a job with MFG in Herndon, Virginia. When I started there, it was quite slow due to some technical difficulties they were having with the product. I was still having problems, especially difficulty sleeping, always unable to stay awake during the day. I lived very close to the office, so once in a while, I'd go home for lunch and take a nap. That job didn't last long at all; it was shut down and dissolved. I ended up getting some small jobs and attended the Goose Creek Ward for church.

It was at Goose Creek that I met my friends, Rocky and JD. These are both solid, outstanding friends that I keep in touch with still today. Goose Creek was one of my favorite wards. Everyone was friendly and helpful. I felt welcome there. Once in a while, I'd go golfing with Rocky and/or play racquetball with JD. I spent my free time traveling with the missionaries and keeping up with my home teaching. At that time, I felt as though things couldn't be much better. I was at my best and on top of my game.

A Man of God

Met that day a stranger kind.
An honest man, now a friend of mine.
We sat a spell in lots of time.
A working man, so sublime.

Extending outward, a helping hand.
With selfless offerings in peaceful sighs.
Eternal wonderment at his command.
Better than the best of men,
He offers up simple prayers,
From deep within his heart, soul, and mind.

A mentor of life's purposeful sway,
That gentlemen's passions pleas
Is all the spirit a man can be.
Angels surround him to take someday,
Prayers were all answered for a delay.
These moments in time are gifts God gave.

Such a righteous man, a wise old sage.
This man of God will never betray.
In this heart, he is here to stay.

Suddenly, things were starting to level out for me, although the jobs were not much to speak of. For a short time, I worked selling mattresses; the manager there stole my commission and I eventually quit. I went back a few times to get him to pay me, but he never did. Well, I worked at a department store for some time selling refrigerators. That was dog-eat-dog; they had too many sales associates for the few customers. Everyone would see how quickly they could approach the customer and steal them away from another salesman. It was incredibly difficult to make any commission. As I said previously, I'm not a salesman.

In my free time, I became involved with N.A.M.I., an organization that provides help for emotionally disturbed individuals and their families. That's where I met Sandy, my second wife, another large mistake. We were giving presentations to first responders on how they should approach emotionally disturbed individuals. Ironically, I would need this for myself one day soon. After introducing Sandy to the church, she showed great enthusiasm. Together, we read church documents, Scriptures, attending church regularly. Quickly, she became baptized and we married. However, everything changed just as quickly. She stopped her medication, becoming extremely agitated and unstable, and started rejecting everything. Church members that showed her nothing but love and support, she now considered enemies. She started constantly admonishing me for reading church materials. Nothing was going good for her. Even though she knew she needed her medication, she refused. She lashed out at me once, telling me she no longer wanted to be married.

I was having a difficult time at work. After several months selling shoes and men's apparel, I was let go. It turns out their scam was to work people for three months at a time. No one lasted more than three months; that way they didn't have to provide any benefits. Anyway, I every day trying to get back into purchasing, constantly ..y computer working with headhunters. Writing resumes, cover letters, and researching companies became my full-time job. I was determined to get back into an administrative position making a decent salary again.

Every Tuesday, I would go to the temple with my friend, Rocky. One particular Tuesday, after working all day to find employment, as was my routine, I began getting myself ready for the temple. Sandy came home and just started sounding off. She was just trying to find anything she could to yell at me. It was, I thought, about a shade in the bathroom that her cat had destroyed. We had a replacement for it, but I hadn't yet replaced it. She just started yelling about how she had had enough of me. It was totally unnecessary and seemingly out of character. I told her that it was enough, and she needed to stop and calm down. She started sobbing and crying and went down to the garage. I just went back to ironing my temple clothes and wondered what I should do. Before I knew what was happening, there was a knock at the door and the police were there. Apparently, she called them saying I had attacked her. I was absolutely flabbergasted; what the heck was going on? I tried telling the female officer that Sandy wasn't taking her meds and required help. All that cop would say is for me to turn around, put my hands behind my back, or she would tase me. She totally refused to listen to anything I had to say. Before I could think straight, I was hauled off to jail, having only my garments and a pair of slacks on. I asked to be able to at least put on some shoes, but that cop absolutely refused.

There I was in jail with no wallet, no cell phone, not even a pair of shoes -- nothing; what the heck was I going to do? After several hours of processing and sitting in jail, I was released. I asked how I was going to get back home and was told it was up to the arresting officer. I had no idea where the jail was even located. They put me out in the back of the jail, and it was now dark, windy, and cold. Not even having shoes, I went back into the front lobby. I didn't even have money for a phone call. So, I sat down and tried to put my thoughts together and figure out what to do.

It was now late in the evening. I asked strangers in the lobby if I could use their cell phone to make a call. To this day, I don't know how or why I remembered the number of brethren at church. Anyway, he came and picked me up right away. I do remember I couldn't even give him directions since I didn't know where I was. The cops refused any help; they wouldn't even look at me. I didn't realize then that they considered me a wife beater.

Once we got back to my house, I wasn't allowed in. The police said there was a restraining order filed against me. If I needed to get something, the police had to be there. Sandy had thrown my clothes out, they were scattered about, up and down the outside steps. It was a total mess. My friend had to get my car keys. I packed up my car with my clothes, then I was out on my own. Having no place to go, I had to sleep in my car.

First thing the next morning, needing some money, I went to the bank. When I got to the bank, I was told my account had been closed two days before. My head was spinning. How could this be? How could a joint account be closed by either one of us? Also, how did Sandy know I would supposedly attack her the day before she accused me? How could anyone treat someone this way? (That's a question I ask every day when watching the news.) So, there I was, out on the street.

My friend, Rocky, having a full house, couldn't help much but let me shower in his basement. I had an interview with a great company in Chantilly, Virginia and ended up getting the job. During the interview, I kept thinking how I hoped they didn't see my car in the parking lot with all my clothes.

After a few days, I reached out to Mike, who had a place locally. Mike rented me a room and that got me off the streets. When I went to court, I was completely railroaded. Not to be totally sexist, the cop was female and so was the judge, the prosecutor, and even my public defender. The only advice my public defender gave me was to just

. I wasn't guilty, so why would I do that? Once in court, , nad Sandy on the witness stand, asking if she said I attacked her. She tried to take it back, but the prosecutor stopped her, not allowing her to speak. They would only allow yes or no answers. I pleaded not guilty, but was convicted anyway. In a matter of minutes, I was convicted without ever being given the opportunity to tell my side. In the entire process from arrest to conviction, I was never allowed to speak. I was put on parole and forced to attend several months of anger management classes. What a way to start my new job.

I had to report to my parole officer (another female) twice a week. The anger management classes were a total farce. The so-called teacher was a sexist woman hater. The class consisted of all men, and they all talked about women as though they were dogs. I was completely uncomfortable. I asked my parole office if I could get out of going. Furthermore, I was a little surprised when I showed up for class; everything I said to my parole officer was repeated back to the instructor. So, the rest of my time in that class, I was considered the enemy. That instructor took every opportunity to use what I had said against me.

On the other side of things, work was going great. The company in Chantilly turned out to be the best job I ever had. Also, it was the best company I ever worked for; it was awesome there. Everyone treated each other with respect and there wasn't any infighting. Other team members actually helped each other out. My supervisor was the best I ever had. She listened and gave good advice that always allowed me to succeed. Her boss seemed to be the same way. The entire atmosphere there was one of comradery and they respected their employees. Quickly, I excelled and started getting more and more responsibilities. I even received a few awards for outstanding work. Getting jobs completed under budget and within the required time frame became my reputation. For a few years, everything was great. I was attending church, golfing with Rocky on the weekends, and even back working out at the gym.

Tranquil Stream

Out on that oasis of green,
It's a warm breeze that sways the trees
Causing them to fold their leaves
Allowing the sun to have its fun
Revealing a tranquil stream.

That water so cold crisp and clean
Lapping along embedded stones
On its way home to a river, wild, wide and deep.
Rushing its way down to an untamed sea.

Oh, Lord! can I stay enjoying these days,
Of that breeze, tangled trees
Reliving that scene of an old country dream,
Down by that tranquil stream?

A position opened up which was located in Elkridge, Maryland. Wanting to be close to my youngest daughter again, I accepted the transfer. I moved to Ellicott City, in the Town and Country apartments. At least this would be closer to Westminster, so perhaps we could visit each other more often. I attended the Ellicott City Ward, which was more difficult than expected. I didn't attend regularly since depression was starting to take over again. Started seeing a psychiatrist, attending group therapy at Sheppard Pratt.

It was at Sheppard Pratt where I met Steve Case. Steve was also bipolar and suffered similar types of anxiety and had anger issues. We instantly were able to relate to each other. What a relief, finally having someone that understood some of what I'd been going through.

At the suggestion of my doctor and friends, I got a dog from the shelter and named him coil. He was a good companion and kept me active, always having to feed and walk him, just giving the attention he needed.

Working away from the main office, in Chantilly, began to be more and more difficult. However, I kept doing what I could to keep things together. Every so often, I had to report to the main office and process documentation for my files. I don't know how I lost control or even why; everything was becoming more difficult.

One day, while attending a meeting with my supervisor going over my account, it happened! Everything completely fell apart. My supervisor was asking questions, I was confidently answering. The problem was, in my mind, I was somewhere else talking about completely different files. When she pointed this out, a rush of reality fell over me. Where the hell was I? It was as though I wasn't even in the same room with her. I know other people were there, but I couldn't even see them. Starting to tremble, I ran out of the office, didn't even know what direction I should take. That office became totally unfamiliar to me. Once again, I was completely lost. My supervisor suggested I go to the hospital and that's what I did. I don't know how I got there, but I remember being admitted for confusion; I didn't know that was even a thing. I couldn't answer any of their questions such as; who the president was, what day it was, anything. So, I was admitted. The only good thing was I quit smoking for good since it was a smoke-free hospital. They offered me the patch, but I refused it. Quitting wasn't difficult for me at all; I just stopped and that was that.

All this happened around the same time my mother passed. She was in an assisted living facility and I tried visiting her. It was always difficult since she never really ever spoke to me as a person. She just would give me updates on how great my brothers were doing, never asking how I was or anything about my children.

When she did pass, I went to the church service. My sister got up and announced names my mother had for each of her children. She called me guileful, and I was so hurt. This woman that never knew me had the nerve to call me guileful. Also, for my sister to stand up in church and repeat it hurt even more. These people, who did nothing but abuse me, were now trying to discredit anything I would ever have to say. This just drove me further into depression with self-hatred. So, there I was, back in the hospital.

I do remember both Rocky and Steve visited me there. Steve gave me the number of his psychiatrist. I was released and, that doctor sent me to have psychological testing done. This was a battery of tests that took several days to complete. I was still out of it and felt as though I was in some dream world. The tests came back with extremely positive results. Still today, when I read that evaluation, I don't understand how and why my mind completely shut down.

Disorganized thoughts, delusional thinking, hallucinations, highly distressed, what a mess. Depression, psychosis, PTSD were all recognized as the cause of my many memory-related issues. All my intellectual functions, including social, occupational, and interpersonal, didn't meet basic standards for functioning normally. All levels of my

were tested as extremely low. Because of this, I was
work and had to apply for SSI disability. This was granted
without any delay; before realizing it, I was now mentally disabled.

More and more, my mental problems kept escalating. While walking my dog, I started falling down. Without any warning, I would just fall down; it always took me by surprise. Steve was walking with us one day and I fell down an incline; he just started laughing. I guess it may have been funny to see, but I wasn't at all amused. Sometimes in the evening, I would drive my car to places, not knowing where I was. Confused, I often left the car for various reasons in my head. I'd somehow find my way home by walking. Once, I went to Hamden in Baltimore and left my car at a 7-Eleven. Through that night, I managed to walk all the way to Ellicott City. I don't know how I did it, but I did. Another time, I thought I drove my car into a Chinese restaurant window, so I walked home. That never happened, but I did leave my car running in the parking lot. When we hunted it down the next day, it was out of gas, the lights still on. It was a Hyundai Sonata that had a tracking device; I only had to call to find its location.

Looking back, I really should not have been living alone. Steve helped me more than anyone did in those days. He didn't live that far away, so I'd often go pick him up. We both had issues; once at the mall in Columbia, we lost my car. Neither one of us could remember where we left it. Thinking it was stolen, we even got the police involved.

The apartments where I lived notified me that they would not renew my lease. With no real explanation, I just figured it had something to do with how often the police were called. Anyway, I ended up making yet another bad decision and bought a trailer in Elkridge, Maryland. Using what money I had left, I paid cash for the place. It wasn't even inhabitable.

Steve and I took that summer to remodel the place, making it livable. Steve is an excellent carpenter, and I had all my experience remodeling the farm house. Even with all the experience we had between us, we still had problems. Both of us had memory issues. So many times, we would get measurements confused. We made many mistakes in cutting material. Still, we got through it, and after all that work, it turned out to be a nice place with a few remaining issues.

Having spent all my money buying the place and now only receiving a small amount of SSI disability, I had nothing left. Therefore, I had to file for bankruptcy. That wasn't that difficult, and I couldn't believe how quick it was. In the process, I lost my car and was stuck in the trailer all the time. I bought a handcart online once, so I could walk to the grocery store and carry my groceries back. First time I tried this, the cart fell apart and my groceries ended all over the street. Very frustrated, I became extremely agitated and angry. Luckily, a neighbor was driving by and offered to help.

I wasn't able to attend church regularly; I didn't see much from anyone there. I got further and further away from my daily Scripture reading. Once again, there was that depression and soon. I couldn't think of much else but suicide. I ended many nights sitting in the dark, contemplating death.

What Is Might?

A continuum of indignation, trapped,
Every fiber of your being, daily tested.
You find the metal of the man is internal strength.
Never will you understand what you don't bother to know.

In all those eyes you clearly see, your arms will forever remain empty.
Whatever stand you make,
Hardheartedness is all loneliness ever gives.
So forsaken, in stillness was beauty.

Yet, it's acid rain that washes this face.
Those words that start out in a stay,
Where all captured off a dead tree.
As they twist and turn, things you say.

Then it's down to this and much less than that.
In defense of the stand you make,
Tonight, you'll not be able to sleep.
So what is might anyway?

After struggling with isolation for some time, my ex-wife Susan offered me a car. That was another of my many mistakes. That car was worthless. I ended up putting several thousands of dollars into it just to get it inspected. I had to take out a high interest loan, since my credit was destroyed. Even after all that, the car was totally unreliable.

Church was pretty much out of the picture then, since I didn't hear from anyone for some time. Having no transportation, I couldn't attend Sunday services. When I did start going back, I had to drive that car very gingerly. In an effort to pay for what I was spending to keep it running, I tried to go back to work.

Delightful Dark Sky

Grave these yards of silent nights,
Tales of woe land winds delight,
Lucid dreams wasted in lost old eyes,
Colorful fields behind rainy gray skies,
Brothers were made in that stage of life.

Sitting for spells with stranger's kind
Years in lots did pass by,
Quenchable thirst of compassion's pries,
Prodigious four corners alert, delightful skies.

Directions point!
From green to gold, to an auburn sky,
Between each word was a gasping sigh.

Through clouded windows, presumptions grew,
Those watchful eyes did suffer you,
When old stories spilled out, wondering why?

There's an empty chair that
Waits ramshackle shame,
Faint was a voice from far, far inside.
Swollen were the tears nevermore will cry,
Fallen by aging contrasts of the dark deep blue sky.

Stubborn and hopeful is static joy,
Cutters stand in wait beyond potter's field,
While silently, trumpeters lay down,
Princes' metals forged for you.

I 'ook a job at a gas station market shop in Elkridge, not far from the trailer. Before I was hired, I told them I couldn't deal with night shift. I was assured that wouldn't happen. The job was fast-paced; the place was always busy. I worked in the kitchen preparing and cooking chicken. I worked hard and it was going well. However, they kept adding on to my responsibilities, giving me more and more shifts. Before long, I was put on the night shift. That didn't last long; the stress was too much. The list of chores each evening began getting longer and longer. The morning shift workers started arriving later and later. This required me to deal with the morning rush. Eventually, I started to crack, and one morning, I just fell apart. I had to get out of that place and I never went back; I was just a nervous wreck.

Having applied for a subsidized apartment in Catonsville about a year earlier, I was notified something was becoming available. Unwittingly, I was looking forward to another change. In spite of all the many address changes over the years, not much was changing in my head. Before I got out of that trailer, I ended up back in the hospital. This time, no one visited me and there was no one I could turn to. No one from my ward was there; I really didn't know anyone anyway. When released from the hospital, I found myself out in their parking lot with no way to get home. Eventually, the police came by and took me back to the hospital. The hospital apparently had a service that arranged transportation to help individuals like me get back home.

By the time I got back home, it was early morning and my anxiety was taking its toll on me. Exhausted, I just sat in my living room for what seemed like days. Confused as to what it was, my mind was scrambled and thoughts were all meshing together.

Beating of a Black Heart

With one sudden, swift blow,
all my lifelong wounds have been reopened.
Now they have been gathered together,
exposed to raw, excruciating pain.
With electrodes firing across my spine, spinning out of control.

There was some excitement of advancing
in darkness with rage, oh yes that rage!
Then the beating of a black heart engaged.
Tried a little smile, but quickly it turned away.
For smiles would always become a grimace
that came from familiar pain.

There was rejuvenation at the expense of being saved.
All formalities whined as each new dawn approached,
New dreadful days.

Questions arose as to survival, rights to life that now expanded
Throughout time and those open gateways.
Then the beating of a black heart did stay.

Walking out into sunlight,
barely living with what was left of what once was…
Someone, or something, pounced, braved a swing.
Hitting me from behind, I wavered through a dense and confused daze.
Wildly swinging out, I caught my enemy.

Avenging this lonesome soul for they were so long in my way.
The beating of a black heart enraged.
In stillness found survivals endurance.

epwalker in some barren ash filled desert,
hat a curse from God above is void of any love.
ters His vengeance within each and every day.
...used as to my history, my crimes, or any sin not yet exposed.

There I prayed, begged, but saw no possible light
For it was blocked out from all sides, only darkness surrounded me.
It was at that moment, then and there...
The beating of a black heart stopped!

CHAPTER 7

That Last Attempt

G iven the opportunity to move into a senior living apartment complex that was subsidized was appealing at that time. I was able to sell my trailer within a week. I almost got what I paid for it, certainly not what I put into it. Thinking it was the best I could do, I took the deal without any hesitation. I moved into senior apartments in Catonsville. It turned out I was only one of two white faces in the entire place. At the time, I didn't think much about that; it didn't bother me at all.

I started back attending services again in Ellicott City. This time, I became more active and started research on my family history, while others in the church often testified on how they got promptings guiding toward family history. I often prayed that I would feel something to help me stay focused; perhaps I could gain a better understanding of my family history. There was nothing, but I kept researching anyway.

Having little to no money, every penny counted. That car my ex-wife gave me finally broke down for good. It left me stranded one day coming home from church on Route 40. I had to junk it and take the money I had from the trailer as a down payment on a Hyundai Elantra. It was a nice car, but my payments and insurance were too high due to my credit history. Struggling to make ends meet, I went to the bishop about my tithing. He advised me to always pay my tithes first and the Lord would provide. So, I took his advice; when I had no food, the church helped feed me. Not really happy about that process, I thought I should at least give it a try.

ments, I was often harassed when walking my dog. from windows, I couldn't see who was yelling, but onplace. There were always the same individuals ...ging out the back door that led to the parking lot. When walking in or out with the dog, I always got nasty comments. I did what I could to just ignore it and go about my business, keeping to myself most of the time. Attending church every week, I even managed to make it to the temple a few times. They shut the temple down for some repairs, and we had to go to Philadelphia. I never made it there and started backing off from church. My home teacher came to visit, offering to help me put together a budget and develop a new résumé. That never happened, and I tried to get a job at a hardware store. I wasn't hired and it really depressed me. Somehow, I needed to get out from the pressure of living month to month and getting food from the church.

I was making weekly visits to a psychiatrist and still taking my medication. I began feeling myself falling back down that hole again. I started being inconsistent with my medication, not certain they had any effect. I started lying to the doctor about how I was doing and if I was taking my meds. Lying to her started getting easier and easier, but the guilt set in. Once again, I was up most nights going out walking the dog and confusion set back in. I started not caring about anything and could only think of how I could end it. I kept in touch with Steve; he always went with me to the bishop's storehouse to get my groceries. That was always an uneasy trip since I felt guilty taking handouts from the church.

What relationship I had with my daughters was fading away. I didn't feel that they cared anything about me, I wasn't a good example for them. Just didn't feel worthy and couldn't think of anything good about myself. My youngest daughter wasn't receptive to anything I had to say. I was invited to her wedding, but it was as though I wasn't even there. Maybe she was embarrassed by me. She never introduced me to any of her friends or his relatives. With the amount of medication I was on, it would have been difficult for me to converse with anyone anyway.

A Few Stray Leaves

A tree stands all but bare, complete,
With hollowed out eyes and hollowed out dreams.
An old, familiar smell will bring you back to what was once new.
Now you're seeing what you've never seen.

There, a window, cold, captures all the heat.
Out there, the battering breeze battles against the brave.
Away from the sun, so far, far away,
Bodies still burn in days of gray.

Those stray leaves hang on, oh so tight,
Conquering work out of their decay,
As each dream conquers moments of time.
These lingering ways are lingering why?

Your paths are scattered as you walk on by.
Dead leaves are flying through pantries
That promise the warmth of July.

A few stray leaves are
Not flouting or bloating,
Standing tall, clinging to the petrified.

Back at the apartment, for some time, was just a place for me to hide. Walking the dog several times a day, I was often approached and asked to give individuals a ride. For the most part, I was successful at keeping to myself. As my depression worsened, one day I finally gave in. A guy that was cutting grass came over and begged me to give him a ride into Baltimore. He promised to give me gas money and seemed somewhat desperate. Now this started a chain of events with others making similar requests. For the life of me, I can't remember names. They all went by street names that never made much sense to me. So, there I was, giving these strangers rides. At first, I didn't know what was going on, but I quickly understood. They were getting me to take them to score drugs.

Before I knew it, people were showing up at my door at all hours, day and night. This woman, Mary, kept showing up, I refused to let her in. I found out later she was a crack whore that had a reputation of giving herself to anyone for a few bucks. Until I understood this, I had no idea what she was talking about. It was as though we spoke different languages. I started getting really irritated with her continuing to bother me. The apartment building was supposed to be secure and only residents should have been able to enter. I went to the front office and complained. Apparently, that woman's mother lived there and she would let her in.

As I was dwindling fast, always depressed and confused, I began to give in. One of the guys I had given a ride to asked to come up to use the bathroom. That was most certainly the beginning of the end. Church was getting further and further out of the picture. I stopped wearing my garments and began to let my guard down. This is one of the most difficult situations for me to write about. I can't remember any names since I was so far gone. For the sake of identifying characters, the guy off the street I'll refer to as Dave and the crack whore

I'll just call Mary. They invaded my life then, and everything changed for the worse.

It would be a total lie if I even attempted to deny using crack cocaine. Being the most insidious drug I've ever done, I let it take control over me. I was already depressed and confused, and it just added to my misery. Before I knew it, my apartment became the place to meet. Dave came over and then refused to leave. I tried many times to kick him out, but he would just eventually return. Mary would show up at all hours, begging to be let in. After refusing to let her in so many times, it seemed I just turned around one day and there she was. Most often, we would all just be sitting around watching TV. Both Dave and Mary had the connections for drugs, they would set up places to meet. I didn't care much either way, feeling that I was just an empty shell of a person.

Having no money and living month to month, my bills were always paid first. Every day, we would always be scrounging around trying to put together a few bucks to buy crack. Dave had a system where he would steal crab meat from B.J.'s and sell it to people in barber shops or anywhere else he could. He tried several times to get me involved, but I could never be a thief.

One day, I received a scam call that I fell for. They offered me a low interest loan, and I only saw a chance to lower my bills. I gave them my bank information, so they could make a deposit. A deposit was made, but they ended up clearing out my bank account. Leaving me with nothing, I couldn't pay any of my bills. My rent was due, I didn't know what to do. I called my friend Mike, he helped me once again. This all depressed me even more. I stopped paying my tithes and backed off from church. I began falling away faster and faster, and then couldn't even take care of my dog. I ended up taking him to a shelter in Ellicott City; I was at a complete loss. I remember being at the shelter with Steve, but I couldn't even speak. He spoke for me, trying to tell them what was wrong. That was so sad; I felt so worthless and just wanted to crawl into a hole.

Suffering Weeds

I know I have lost
For the pain it cost,
Was all paid out in vain.

So I'm hanging my head,
Dragging my feet,
Falling down in these suffering weeds.

Looking back up,
Not finding any love,
So I'm hoping and praying for belief.

Will ever there be more
Then lonely days by the score,
And waking and walking in these suffering weeds?

After falling for that scam, everything got even worse. It is so diffi-cult for me to even think about those days; trying to write these words is nearly impossible. Not having any money at all, I started letting others use my car. They paid for my gas and gave me a few extra bucks. This was just another bad decision I didn't care about. My feeling was it would all be over soon, for my life was about to end. Dave became comfortable sleeping on my couch. He would walk around in the apartment nude, claiming he was straight. I didn't under-stand what or why he was doing what he did. I often found myself just staring at him. He was very well-endowed, I didn't feel the least bit attracted to him. I really couldn't feel anything anymore.

So, there I was always in my apartment, which was furnished very well. I always kept my living areas nice and clean, but even that was getting more and more difficult. My car, which was relatively new, was being abused by strangers. At first, they returned it on schedule, but before I knew it, I was up every night waiting for them to return it. My feelings about that were mixed. I'd say each time was the last time, but I always gave in. I was living in a nightmare and wasn't certain what I could do to escape.

Crooked Vultures

Crooked vultures with
Useless talons still carry
Remnants of death across
A blood-stained sky.

Cinnamon haze settled down
On iron scaffolds that measure
Shadows revealing the length of
Life remaining in each day.

With my shameless manifest,
I stood wallowing in bagged and
Tagged resistance, with little
Restraint and nothing to say.

Out in the distance between
What once I knew as love,
The wait continued and
It all faltered and fell into a
Continuum of common indignation.

So that life, life that hates to plead,
Begged to borrow grace from living things.
Truly, it is only survival of the fittest that
Could succeed, breathe, and continue to be.

All those crooked bone twisted,
Fingers extending outward were without cause.
While each cell mutated and
Forced this aging man to loudly scream, it
Reverberated down within the marrow of my soul

Yet, pain became another lost feeling,
Never mentioned; it came on without blame.
And I could only look at each and every scene,
To diagnose the problems never meant to be seen.

Not learning lessons from past visions, or
exploring my life's architectures that now,
Dress in monogram prints while they
Dragged dead dogs along narrow paths.

Found myself wishing and hoping for a youthful
Corpse which became my only pleasant
Memory, and only on sunny day graves.

There I was lying in bed one night waiting for my car to be returned, and it hit me. This all had to end, it had to end at that moment. I got up and took a bottle of trazodone, which was almost full (since I wasn't taking it regularly) and just started swallowing them, one after the other. I sat down in the living room with a bottle of water and just stared out into the abyss, swallowing them. Dave eventually took notice and started asking what I was doing. He kept telling me there was nothing wrong with me and I needed to stop. Eventually, he called 911 and the police showed up with an ambulance. The paramedic kept asking how many pills I swallowed, but I just couldn't say anything. They gave me some charcoal and pumped my stomach. When we got to the hospital, I still couldn't say a thing.

I Am a Stone

Today I'll dive deep,
Make not a ripple,
Make not a peep.

For now, I'm a stone,
And now I can't speak.

To be a stone is what I must be,
For anything else,
Would be weak.

So today I won't …
Cry out, write, or speak.

I'll remain a stone…
A little larger than sand,
Still…nothing at all unique.

Once I arrived at North-West Hospital in Baltimore, I was stuck. Not able to speak, I could only look at whomever was talking to me. I didn't understand what they were saying. They kept trying to take my blood and couldn't find a vein. At least a half a dozen people came in and tried, but finally they gave up. Here I was, once again alone in a hospital room, the last place I wanted to return to, yet there I was. After a while, I started talking and gave the nurse all the information he needed. I cooperated with everything they asked; my experience with those places helped me understand that it would be best if I did. One of the male nurses told me I was the best patient they had, since I gave them no trouble. I know he meant it as a compliment, but I was even more saddened by it. Being an expert in a mental hospital stay wasn't what I ever wanted for me. There, I was getting along with everyone.

I was there a few days and remembered that the door lock on my apartment door wasn't working. I called the apartment's front office and had maintenance go check. Both Dave and Mary were there, and I asked the head of maintenance to get them to leave.

This hospital stay became my longest. I called my youngest daughter in Westminster, but she refused to even visit. She said she wanted nothing to do with me. Once again, since I wasn't dead, I had to pick myself up, just do something. There was a doctor and social worker assigned to me. The doctor just filled me up with medication and the social worker said I could no longer live on my own. She said I needed to move into a group home. They would have a care person who would administer my medication. It was a no-win situation; they wouldn't discharge me until I agreed. They said it was my choice, yet they gave me no other option.

My brother Bruce and his wife, Kathy, came to visit and helped me get out. I agreed to move to a home in Westminster, feeling the need to be close to my daughter, Erin; even though she wanted nothing to do with me, I still had to try. Bruce spoke with my doctors and therapist and went with me to a few of my appointments. He and Kathy were very involved for a short time.

When I arrived back at my apartment to make moving arrangements, it was all trashed. My place was totally ransacked while I was in the hospital. Even though I felt I knew the crackheads that did it, I had no proof. It was a disaster; they stole my complete entertainment section: a large-screen TV and the cherry wood and glass stand it was mounted on. My stereo was gone, yet they left some of the components. My iPod, iPad, my Bose speakers, everything was gone. What they couldn't steal, they smashed, destroyed. My glass coffee table and end table were all smashed. I had nothing left but a large mess to clean up. They even stopped up the toilet and let it run over. Water was running down the apartment under me. Maintenance came in when I wasn't there, but only turned off the water. They didn't lift a finger to help me with anything.

My car was missing, so I had to track it down and get it back. Erin reluctantly came and helped me get it back. When I got it, there was a lot of damage as if it was involved in an accident. Naturally, the guy I got it back from knew nothing about its condition. So, I just got the keys and took it home.

At the apartment, several people helped me: my brother Bruce, my home teacher from church, and Steve Case. I never saw those crackheads again. I asked around at the apartments if anyone saw or heard anything and, of course, no one admitted it. This was a secured building with cameras and cipher locks, yet no one saw a thing. An entire entertainment section, 42-inch TV, carried out and no one saw a thing. I can't help but think that had everything to do with the color of my skin. It wasn't my first time being the only white in a Black neighborhood. I always let the derogatory comments go and just ignored them. But this was just much too much. I was at my lowest and they took full advantage. Anyway, it took a lot of hard work to make that move. I could not have made it without the help of Erin, my brother, and friends. I was definitely just going from God's gift of strength to strength, maintaining the best I could. But I was still in a fog, perhaps from being over-medicated. Since I was still breathing, I felt I had no choice but to make things better. How, I wasn't certain; I just kept moving forward.

Brave the Wind

So you nettled bath and fast,
And exposed a providence of sin.
You still must brave the wind.

As those illiterates, inarticulate,
with wandering souls surround.
history does repeat.
Over there it goes on again,
Turning back those barbarians,
Rediscovered old concepts,
with that scholarship of religion.

Still, you must brave the wind.
So listen to the ancient sounds,
Of all those troubadours,
Receive your healing and understand
You must still brave the wind.

After losing everything (once again), I moved into the group home in Westminster. My room was in the basement of a two-story home, very close to the busy Deer Park Road. They took all my money, leaving me with only a few hundred dollars I needed for medication. Once a month, I was able to go to Walmart and get toiletries, not much else. I lost my car; since I could no longer pay insurance or my loan, it was repossessed. I even lost my cell phone since I could not pay the bill. I had to rely on getting rides from another patient in the house. One very cold winter day, he gave me a ride to the health department and left me there. I had to walk over seven miles back to the house. On Route 32, there is always very busy traffic and no sidewalks. It was cold, I was very upset, foolishly thinking they would come look for me, but no one did. When I finally got back, it was getting dark and my rider wasn't there. I found out later he went to Pennsylvania to see his girlfriend and forgot about me.

The place was horrible; my room was small and dirty. They gave me an old twin bed that sloped down; it was difficult to lie in. I had to share a bathroom with everyone else. It was always filthy. The shower never drained properly, so you would always end up standing in several inches of dirty water. Also, they had a roach problem that went on for way too long. I would have nightmares and hallucinations. My recurring nightmares were having roaches crawl up my nose and I couldn't get them out. I dreamt that several times and I woke up screaming, only to be yelled at by whomever was working that night. Also, I had hallucinations of being in a high rise building on the top floor in a room, trapped. I would climb all around, trying to find my way out, certain it was true. When I got a glimpse of reality, I didn't know which was true. After having those hallucinations, my room would be in a wreck by morning. No one there paid any attention as to what was going on with me. I tried to get out and walk, but they would not let me even go up the driveway. That house was so close to the road, it was just too dangerous.

Others in the house had emotional problems much worse than mine. The people running the place were disorganized and didn't seem to care about our well-being. They had trouble keeping employees. Supposed caregivers came from Baltimore and were not qualified to care for anyone. They were to prepare our meals and issue our medication, and also take care of the individuals that couldn't take care of themselves.

The food was every bit as bad as everything else there. They never fixed a meal from scratch; it was always cheap, highly processed crap with no nutritional value whatsoever. In the evening, they would give us snacks that were garbage. The one thing they said they had a handle on was issuing our medication. The meds were always locked up, yet mine were often stolen. Why anyone would want psychotropic and anxiety meds is beyond me. There I was, so many times, not getting my required medication. There was nothing I could do about it; when complaining, it went on deaf ears. They never investigated who stole the meds.

Then one day, I contacted the church missionaries and found my way back to church. I was assigned to the Sykesville Ward and my home teachers were Brother Ronald Gilbert and Brother Myers. Both were extremely generous individuals that made certain I had a ride to church every Sunday. In fact, over the next two years, I never missed a Sunday, thanks to Brothers Gilbert and Myers. I went back to wearing my garments and reading Scriptures. I tried to be active in other ways, but that was difficult. I had no car and no money, and with the meds, my thoughts were often fogged and confused. I still kept trying and trying my best just to survive each day.

An Old Rose

I caressed that rose,
Until its thorns dug down deep,
Causing me to bleed.

I captured all its beauty,
And its aromatic scent so sweet,
Invoked magical memories.

As each petal withered
And fell into decay,
Tears of rage flowed relentlessly,
With all that blood around my feet.

Now wading ankle-deep in regret,
For never will I hold another rose sweet,
In anything but distant dying whisper
Of a now forgotten rhapsody.

In early December, the manager gave us all notice that we had to vacate that house by the end of the month. Here I was once again with no money, nowhere to go, and soon to be out on the street. I was, to say the very least, panicking. What could I do? So, I prayed and prayed. Then I begged the manager to help me. I went to the Housing Department in Westminster and the Bureau of Aging, and everywhere I could by taking the bus. No agency would help me, even though all my money was going to my living situation. They said I was over the limit for getting any help. So I was out of luck, except for my last resort, which was getting help from the church.

My Creator

My Creator is omnipotent,
He is above all there is and or ever was.
He holds true dominion over all worlds,
Of yesterday, today, and beyond.

My Creator taught me how to speak,
But He does not tell me all I can say.
He gives me gifts and blessing of sight,
Strength, and willful might in mindful ways.

He said to me, walk upright,
Stay free, for it was my ancestors that paid with blood,
stood in bondage,
And were once held as slaves.

My Creator said I have purpose,
An empathetic centered seer, feeling
All the love as well as each grain of suffering;
Caused by our worldly ways.

My Creator tells me stay faithful, for
No one could ever impute or stand
Charge against the man
That I've become today.

He said He loves us all in equal amounts,
But different yet still in equal ways.
My Creator allows me to fill this blank page,
Until it holds all my soulful staves.

M y prayers were quickly answered: the house manager took me to an assisted living facility in Finksburg, Maryland (Master's Haven). They agreed to rent me a furnished room that included two meals a day and three on weekends. Although they wanted more than I was already paying, I didn't have much choice. The church helped me pay the security deposit, and Brother Ron and Brother Dave helped me move. It was the first of January; it was cold and snowing that day. As it turned out, this place wasn't much better than the last place, although it didn't have the roaches and mice, so in that respect, it was better. The room was much larger, but the bathroom was very small and way down the hall. I didn't have to share the bathroom with anyone else, so that was a plus. The food wasn't much better than the place I had just left. Also, they never met their part of the bargain as to the number of meals. They had a large turnover with help, and they would often forget about me. I had a small refrigerator Bruce loaned me; I kept some food in there to offset when meals didn't show up.

Since this was an assisted living facility and I didn't require assistance, they left me alone. In fact, I was told to stay away from the other residents and keep to my room. The bed was a worn-out twin and quickly became an issue for my back. I developed severe back issues and had to go to pain management and physical therapy. The pain was excruciating and shot down my spine to my leg (It was my sciatica). At one point, I literally had to crawl down the hall to use the bathroom. I was in so much pain that they gave me oxycodone. Not wanting to rely on pills, I didn't take many.

With nothing to do, I started to go to the senior center where I played billiards and had lunch, just for something to do. My brother, Bruce, gave me a Fitbit and I started walking every day. I achieve the ten-thousand-steps-a-day challenge right away. Before long, I was at twenty thousand steps. I walked everywhere I could, every day, regardless of the weather. Walking, for me, was a blessing and a cure for some of my depression. The only problem was, I had to walk alongside Route 140, a very busy highway with no sidewalks, but I just kept walking.

I needed to get out of that place, since I was always alone and had nothing to do but watch TV; I just had to get out. Having applied to some other apartments earlier, I started calling around with the new phone my brother hooked me up with. He and his wife helped me so much in those days. I really appreciate them. Anyway, I called and tried to find some place to live, anything. I found out from a friend at the Senior Center that Timber Ridge had some apartments available.

Surrounding Angels

Tripping all over angels from above,
Stuck in each moment of that cry of the dove,
Lifted by the weight of howling winds,
This life would be in shambles if not for that friend.

There was something she said that you kept in your head.
But there is a place you must go instead.
Born to plunder through eternal wonderment,
Go straight back down to that old hotel.

Walk back down to those tracks again.
This world around you is as good as it gets.
Each specter reveals truth in the eyes of an old friend.
As you're bound and gagged in that obscure self-importance.

It's unjustifiable, that pride which scatters, ignores,
And flies away, away on by...

CHAPTER 8

Still Not Finished

My one-year commitment at Master's Haven in Finksburg was about to end. Bruce called to see what I wanted for Christmas, and I told him nothing except to get an apartment somewhere. After that, it would be several years before I heard from him again. For some reason, he stopped returning my calls. (To this day, he doesn't answer.) I called over to Timber Ridge and spoke with the manager; she was responsible for renting and helping with all the paperwork. Anyway, she confirmed something would be available. However, she would only call me when a studio was available. I questioned her on that since I put in for a one bedroom; I guess I was too anxious as I just let it go. She said that's just the way it was. I wanted to get out of Finksburg so bad, I'd take whatever she had.

I ended up with a studio apartment, which wasn't bad. There was a lot of light, it was clean, and was a place where I could once again start over. I couldn't have done it if not for the help from the church; they helped with the security deposit, as did Brother Ron and Brother Dave. Additionally, Brother Link helped out; he was also from the Sykesville Ward. Brother Link would often take me to the store and my doctor's appointments when I was in Finksburg. He is still a friend that I feel I can always talk with. For some time, that apartment worked out well for me.

I had to get the rest of my teeth pulled; this was something I had started a few years earlier. They were pretty bad off and the dentist said they could save a couple; the cost for me was prohibitive.

When I finally got the last tooth out, the person that did it was inexperienced and made a mess. Poison from the tooth got in my bloodstream and I got cellulitis. Within three weeks, I gained 87 lbs. and had to go to the emergency room several times. At first, my doctor couldn't figure out what was wrong. He sent me to a cardiologist because he suspected I had congestive heart failure. I became so heavy and always out of breath so that I couldn't even do the stress test. It was in the emergency room that they diagnosed me with cellulitis. They kept me there until I lost some of the water weight. I still haven't lost all the weight I had gained then. The cellulitis proved to be very difficult to get rid of. My feet were so swollen I couldn't put shoes on. Everything became more and more difficult. After many rounds of antibiotics, I finally got it under control, but it took many months. Right after cellulitis, I caught the flu; that knocked me completely out for several days. Doctor bills began piling up, taking everything that I had.

I started back with the church, assigned, this time, to the Westminster Ward. Not having a car limited what I could do. I always had to rely on others to give me rides to Sunday service. I couldn't pay my tithes and felt guilty and uncomfortable there.

In the LDS Church, you are given a calling if the local leadership receives promptings or inspirations. Yet, no such calling ever came my way. To be recognized as having a calling, you need to be set aside, but that never happened for me. At the very minimum, you are assigned other members that you are to minister to. This never happened, even though I had several conversations with the priesthood president. I was never welcomed in that ward. I assumed it was due to my being single. Also, I confided in the bishop of my same-sex attraction and that haunted me. He never spoke with me again. The church maintains they are all-inclusive, but that is not my experience or perception. I had to deal with local realities. If asked, this all will be denied; they will say the right words. Still, they never included me in much of anything. Being asked to watch the door during sacrament is not inclusive of anything. My situation is a gray area; they just didn't wish to deal with me. In fact, my membership records with that ward were deleted. I'm no longer assigned to any ward or have any calling, for I'm just insignificant to everyone there. As it turns out, this was a blessing. Being deleted from the LDS church, forced me to investigate a true church and I found that at Westminster Baptist church.

The Whispering Wind

The turning leaves
The screaming trees
The fading green decay
The branch in storms that break

The stance it all must make
The clatter of our understanding
The what, this world will pay
The majestic colors of spring

The weave above the trees
The smell of fall's burning leaves
The evening sun that speaks
The murmur of a forest of trees

The smiles these things bring
The sweetness of this world
The God in everything

Gray

I know gray,
Early morning of summer's skies,
The air's still, small chill,
Masking a humid day.
My cleaves for erudition,
Rains sharp boldness,
Objects of fluid dreams.

I know this gray
Membrane that fogs these old eyes,
Old stones, the color of,
the hardness of the streets,
Winters bare trees,
A window someday I should clean,
Temple distinguishing a man's age

I know this gray
Manic hallucinations afflictions,
The matter of this brain,
Dust mixed in white paint,
Oh yes, do I know this gray!

So, my bills were being paid, but having nothing left and living month to month got the best of me. I was still seeing a psychiatrist for my anxiety and depression medication. They were so expensive, I started to take myself off of them. During this time, I was seeing my general practitioner and as a result of my blood work, he noticed I had elevated PSA. Therefore, he sent me to a urologist. This started an entire chain reaction of more tests, procedures, and the bills, bills I could not afford but kept piling up.

Sleep has always been a problem for me, and the stress caused by my poor health made it all much worse. Or has stress made my health worse? It is all related; lack of sleep causes many evil things. I spent every night cooking and cleaning and also writing whenever I got the urge. I started making cakes and gave them to my neighbors. I'd take them down to the social room and it quickly became a thing. The women there seemed to appreciate it; I made some friends in the process. That was spoiled when they started expecting it. They started making demands such as what I should make the next time. I became extremely discouraged and had to stop baking altogether. Looking back, it was the lack of sleep that really caused my irritation. After several weeks without sleep, I started hearing voices and hallucinating. I remember looking in my closets for a leash to walk my dog. After tearing everything out of my closet, I looked around and my dog was gone. A cold chill came over me when I realized he was not there at all. I had given him to that shelter years before. But his being there was so real that I just sat down on the floor in fear.

Death's Cold Whisper

Death's cold whisper will not let me be,
It's getting louder and louder these days, you see,
Like how those shadows of my past,
Will not stop following me.

Anchored in this living hell,
I begged for new beginnings,
Asking only for the darkness,
Finally, to recede.

Once I traced the Lord's footsteps,
Under the waves of a now barren sea,
Followed them for decades,
They lead me here to Thee.

In all my twisted tales,
One truth does still prevail,
His goodness is in that light,
I wait for it to shine on me.

Exhausted, battled, bruised, and beaten,
Where is my time? Where is my relief?
Death's cold whisper will not let me be.

The results came back for the biopsy on my prostate. They found something; it was very early and the doctor assured me they could take care of it quickly. The thing is even though I was worn out from lack of sleep, I'd been suicidal all those years, the word "cancer" still put a scare in me. On top of that, the COVID pandemic hit a short time after and everything changed, not much so in my reality, for it is just another annoyance and concern. My doctor bills were getting way out of control, so I looked to the VA for my medical needs.

Started seeing VA doctors for my mental health issues. They got me involved with video conferencing four days a week. The primary doctor at the VA suggested I stay with my urologist since they had already started treating me.

As for my day-to-day life, I was still having difficulty sleeping. I was cooking elaborate dishes almost every day. I would take some over to my neighbor, Debbie, across the hall. We quickly became good friends. I shared my poetry and cooking with her and we would talk for hours. I told her upfront that I was not interested in a relationship at that time. We had several frank discussions on the subject. She also had her own issues, but it seemed we really enjoyed each other. We had a lot of common interests and similar points of view. I really admired Debbie and after some time, I started developing some strong feelings for her. She moved, but we kept in touch. In fact, we even saw more of each other. I'd take her out several times a week, we texted and/or talked every day. As soon as I started feeling comfortable with her, it stopped! She went away with an old guy on a motorcycle. How silly is that? The thing is, she didn't even talk to me about it; she just texted me and that was the end of that. Admittedly, I took it personally and was distraught.

The winter that year was particularly rough. I'd still take my morning walks, but it was icy and cold and very slippery.

Fallen Mercury

A day in sullen movements, snow did fall this way.
Mercury fell, arriving late, awake half dead,
I lifted my head to another day.
Collecting thoughts that filled my attic by forsaking logic
and its mournful weight.

Still could not bring back that light, into this day,
shortened by winter's lasting ways.
Each frozen breath is now taken as a refuge from some suicides retreat.
All now expelled within this ghost-filled wind from dusk to dawn's
escape, and all farewells are Not well received, even in the bitterness of
cold which now stands naked and exposed to history.

These are desperate measures, trying to find warmth in words
stolen from strangers' dreams.

Each faultless step advances, to depths of emptiness,
in frozen death so willingly.
These philosophical calls beg to play on for merriment,
speech that someday may win a victory.
As loneliness and fallen mercury together surrender,
each step today I take,
They defend against that loneliness of these
cold nights and shortened, dense days.

Unwillingly and slowly, she fuels the fires that burn bright inside my
mind, billowed with those Once fearful and long forgotten tears shed.
This season of joy, my season of a thousand sorrows,
is howling at coldness today.

Still, seeing her face too easily and being remembered
in the banks of snow-blind days

It is much too much to take.
I'm still scraping ice from each vice of those old ways, such as wanting
companionship, a greedy need of human kindness defined as humanity.
Perhaps some belonging or acceptance from this fragile human race?
Like the virtue of a rose, the loyalty of a dog, still I dwell
within these gates, staying in wait.

But the mercury has fallen; I rise from my bed each day unfulfilled …
as it is, everyone has Gone away, no change I made
could ever get them to stay.
I do somehow offend … as I identified them with blank faces,
so they can all just walk away. That Stain of her anger echoes
and melts each faithful and beautiful snowflake,
Still, I take in all they gave.

The drifts of the snow, those eyes all inflamed,
reach out to each and every frozen angel's wing.
With knowledge of how I know that this is all so, why it's given to a
lowly servant that has fallen With mercury in degrees?
Still, I walk on each day.
Mercury has fallen in so many ways.

There I was again, another failed relationship, many health issues, and sleepless nights that lead to endless difficult, confused days. One of my many doctors once told me I had a bad picker. He explained that I was picking sociopaths and narcissists, due to my early development, always trying to please those that will never be satisfied. He added that I will always be disappointed and frustrated when the outcome is inevitable, due to my bad picker. At that point, I was feeling hopeless again. It seemed as though I would never get a good night's sleep.

The only thing I had to sleep on (in my studio apartment) was a large recliner. At first, this was OK; if I did sleep, it was no more than two or three hours. Definitely, that was not enough sleep to stay functional throughout the day. For me, this had just become a way of life.

Both my doctor and therapist suggested I keep my sleep area separate from my living area. I called the manager at the apartment complex to see if they could put me in a one bedroom. They refused to even entertain the idea, even with my doctor's note, which they refused to look at it, saying to move me was cost prohibitive. It became obvious that I would have to find another place if I ever wanted to sleep again. Not having the funds required, due to my medical bills, was so frustrating, I could hardly stand it. I did start looking and applying for places nearby.

At that time, I was in touch with my brother, Michael, every day. To help both of us get out and to become active, I started taking him places. We went to the Senior Center to play billiards, out to lunch, and on small hikes. Every day, I'd ask if he wanted to do anything, but more times than not, he would say no. He is on 100 percent disability with the VA and requires assistance due to his mental capacity. His short-term memory is extremely limited, just about nonexistent.

The woman he lives with has complete control over him. She controls all of his finances and medications. She is his advocate at the VA. While he is very lucky to have her, she is overbearing and abusive. I've witnessed her yelling and lashing out at him many times. I know she means well. Like everyone, she has her own problems. The problem is, she will not get the help she needs. She stays in bed almost every day watching TV and on her computer (tablet). He spends his time in the living room watching TV. Anyway, it's just so hard to see them wasting their lives away.

They kept pushing me to get in a new place and offered to help me financially. I really didn't want to do it, but I did it anyway. I found the place I'm in now; it's absolutely wonderful. It's more like a cottage than an apartment. No one is above or below me. I have my own private entrance and a patio. The rooms are spacious and, yes, finally I have a bedroom. I never could have done it without my brother's help. Even though I've paid them back, I can never really repay what they have done for me emotionally. For the first time in my life, I'm feeling positive, I think I can really make it this time. The love I've always had in my heart is still there. Through everything, I've tried to stay true to the love deep inside me. It's been with me before birth, and I expect to carry it on as I pass away. For now, I'll continue to write about what I feel and see every day.

Strength of Something to Say

Dragons rip flesh still, no longer flinch we will,
It's history prior to birth,
So said Cicero, so hear this, there is,
Strength of something to say.

A witness in God, declaring He heard,
The whispering wind of humanity,
Feeling unworthy, still He speaks, with
Private bitter strength.

As a child, tortured he was,
As a man, he fell through many floors,
At birth, he felt cursed, in retrospect
It could have been worse.

Take it from this man that bleeds too much,
Our greatness they can never touch,
So take His hand and He'll steal a hug,
You already have His love.

Overcome that viper, exodus the darkness,
For friends are our armor, words can steady our swords. Nothing says
vengeance, there is no revenge. Though never apologies admitting their
crimes, really there is only One that we need to bestow us pride.

So bless that friend that touches nothing save,
the heart of God's child they so betrayed.
Thus, we can refute imposing dragons indignantly.
As we stand on this orb and together make,
Our platforms' speech compassionately.

Such is the strength of something to say,
With that benevolent foundation we build
Understanding. We can undo those nautical knots,
Binding new, with a truce, and devotion to God.

Early Morning

Out there is a gold crescent moon
Plastered to a black satin sky,
Countless are the stars that
With each step toward dawn
Quickly fade away.

A warm humid breeze laughing,
As it cuts through the bushes,
And cuts through the trees.
Finally, I realize that breeze
Isn't laughing at me.

All that jubilation destroys
The reasons for tangled
Voices in those trees.

An old man said he saw us,
Walking across the river.
To another time, to new
Found pleasantries.

We did leave our homes,
For they drove us away.
We traveled the shoulders
Of our future and respected
History of those sacrifices made.

Deep in our hearts, we know
And always knew what
Was our need.

A Morning to Be Remembered

Today, although so cold, the air was crisp and clean.
The sun was rising slowly, reflecting, glittering
On fall's red leaves.

A crow on a crooked branch announced my advance onto that scene.
To my right in a field still filled with frost, yet still green.
White tail deer stood, watching this stranger,
The intruder, that was me.

In a romantic dance, they slowly turned and trotted away.
Oh, what a morning such as this, so awake, observant of everything.
What a gift to store these things in a memory.

A feeling of gratitude to be blessed in such a beautiful, enticing way.

A Scattering Leaf

On my way today, on the path I did take,
Was startled by a scattering leaf.
Within a second split between a pause,
A deep breath that I had to take.

It was a roller coaster of emotion, from
Fear which drew some heat, quick to relief.
Left with self-awareness, much
Embarrassment that, as quickly, did overtake.

After all, how silly to be startled by a scattering leaf.

When My Brother Speaks

When my brother speaks, his words are trapped
In echoes of my earthly father's speech.
He often issues out comments, demands,
Meant to hurt, meant to cut you deep …
When my brother speaks, it's to him more
Superior, more intelligent than anyone else could be.

So listen, pay close attention, be mindful of all that
Deep-seated history.
Consider who said what and to whom.

When it was first struck in violent, hateful lashings.
When my brother speaks, does he even realize he is a
Part of that history oh so often found to repeat?

Can we help my brother to speak in concise honesty?
Will he ever offer up the truth of what he really wants to say?
Let us help break those chains, for once in this lifetime
give him a voice to speak compassionately.
When my brother speaks …

Did I Save a Soul?

In rejecting the natural man, did I save a soul?
All I see today as I stand is the last exit before me.
Where are the promises I heard from you oh so long ago?
Those that worship in Your church have all turned their backs

When I revealed the true nature of what destroyed
This mind, destroyed this body, and perhaps destroyed this soul.
So here I am, a fat old man, woefully wallowing in the nature of what I am.
Will you deny this tortured, ragged being before You
The rights to enter the halls of Your mansion?

In all my struggles with that natural man, who lost many,
many battles, I still stand. However,
Gripping on to each strength of moral confusion.
I regained consciousness in bitter contempt for all the required sacrifices,
All I gave in bloodletting for You.

The nature of what I am lies wrapped around a dying heart.
Still, I admit to a befuddled state of who and what.
Out there in the distance, it all seems black.
I can't keep my eyes from turning back.

My soul's intention was, once before I left, to learn to fly.
Now I'm more grounded, and each day's long shadows
Linger and blanket this place where I stand.

Now here I bow again, to You, and all I don't understand.
For in each and every imaginable ending,
You still made the man that I am...

This Has to End

At some point, this all has to end.
I can, as proven to myself, make any sacrifice.
Giving up any vice, but what will remain?
Will I go back to my vision from years past?
Becoming a burning, screaming, bleeding piece of wasted wood.

Out there, will I just be left floating in a massive void of nothingness?
Be forgotten by the universe, and left being extinguished?
Like snuffing out a cigarette or die out in a pile of ash?

For a time, I covered up and muted my screams
In rooms with padded walls, forgetting the anguish and all that pain.
Once with alcohol, then drugs and explicit sex games,
All to cover up hurt plied by those
I should have been able to trust.
Never showing an ounce of love.

The pain, yes pain even here today remains;
I tried all your remedies, gave myself to religion,
Which I committed to quite seriously.
Read and discussed all those Scriptures
That were written by who knows whom,
And in what manner?

However, I prayed and prayed, in your temple,
Made all the sacrifices partaking those ordinances.
Just to be devalued, disgraced, then deleted
As punishment due to some judgment
From others that claim not to judge.

Complied with those doctors
And their mood alterations and psychotropics.

They didn't stop anything,
Never took away the suicide or the addictive purpose.
Only kept out the realities of life
And its daily deceptions with mundane ways.

Now that all has, again, been taken from me,
(Not that I ever really had a thing), what is there left?
Where do I go from here?
What move do I make that will ever be true enough?

During each morning's run, I feel pain
In my back, my legs, arms
But lie, saying to myself,
Keep moving on, keep digging in,
And somehow life will have been won.
Where do I place this bus load of misguided faith …?

Each burden that I received was not a gift,
Yet, that is just what they have been masked to be.
Now, I have to question and take issue with everything.
No longer accepting anything that
On surface, it appears to be.

To what extent and what are the implication
Of what that all means?
What is it that will finally kill and devour
The remaining spirit of me?

As my nerves cut through my bones
And the sinew depletes,
Where is the purpose,
Why was there ever
Someone such as me?
But for now.

These Freezing Hands

With these freezing hands
And this bloody face, I'll
Keep skating into the bitter
wind above this frozen place.

If you've come to watch me
falter and/or fade away,
You misunderstand the
Eminent spirit which remains.

That, my long-forgotten friend,
Would be your mistake.
Once tethered and held back,
With new guidance, I'm on
A new path to a home of purity
Of sight, sound, and love that will stay.

Though not fully witnessed,
Each little glimpse sets me free.
So often I cried out, begged, and prayed.
Like a cloudy day at times, there
Is a break, a ray,
Giving hope for a sunny day.

When climbing out of this valley,
I'll continue striving
and reach that pinnacle,
Of all that ever was or
All that ever could be.

Leaving nothing for chance,
Out of this world of man,
I will find a place of peace.

CHAPTER 9

A New Healing Path

My daughter, Christine, has become my greatest ally and source for detailed knowledge on both my mental and physical health. Before she introduced me to the concept of narcissism, I had no idea what that was. I started reading books, which she suggested, and watched multiple podcasts on the subject. Each time I read or heard something, it was as though my reasons for past suffering became clearer and clearer.

All those years, I kept blaming my emotional problems on my childhood. The facts are now in, the true cause of my trauma was by and large due to my narcissist wife. The horror and psychological games she inflicted were so evil and came out of an entity of darkness so deep in the bowels of cruelty that not the devil himself would dare to enter. The more I educate myself on the subject, the closer to understanding I'm becoming. How someone I loved so much could issue out punishments and purposefully continually hurt me in efforts to destroy me, without any regard for basic human kindness, still is difficult for me to conceive.

But the facts are all there and truths are piling up. From the very beginning of our relationship, she put her sadistic plan into action. What I now know is called the "love bomb" and that was what she did to me. Soon after we married, she stopped allowing me to even kiss her. There was absolutely no passion from her that quickly, and I became the aggressor, wanting love from her, I now know she could never give. All those years, I kept hope that things would change if I just did this or that for her. I became a slave to her every desire and command. Sex from her was just something she used, always for her advantage. I always did whatever she wanted. Not once in the entire relationship did she make any effort to do or say anything to please me. Honestly, if I really analyze that part of our life, I would have been better off with a blow-up doll or just a pile of rocks.

I wanted a loving family and to raise children in an atmosphere of love that I never had as a child. She, however, selfishly wanted to keep getting high by smoking pot, saying the hell with the rest of the world. I was just an obstacle but, at the same time, a vehicle for her to achieve whatever she wanted. My wants, desires, and concerns meant absolutely nothing to her. As my love was so blind, I kept trying and trying with never an ounce of support. The really sick thing is, being with her was still better than my childhood, even with the abuse—I didn't know any better—for at least I got some attention. Although it was all negative and unfulfilling, it was still attention, which was more than anything I had ever known.

While each night was filled with nightmares,
my days were filled with dreams.
Dreaming of the day she would find a way to love me.
Dreaming that together we could grow and make ourselves
a happy, loving family.

Angry and Tired

Getting angry and tired,
Today I'm feeling weak.
Unlike Jacob Marley rattling
Those chains,
I can't put
Together two links.

It is so hard to make that noise,
When all you want to do is sleep.

In my head,
I keep hearing:
You there! Boy! ... hey man,
Why don't you ever
Smile and show
Some teeth?

Never did I dance,
Just couldn't keep that
Native beat.

Everything is serious
When you've been hurt and
Cut so deep.

Forever is some concept
For those born
In delight so sweet,
Not the one relegated
To endless misery.

Bitterness becomes
Seductive when you've
Never tasted
Anything sweet.

All I'm after now is
A set of fresh clean sheets.

A Bullet Lodged

With a bullet lodged
In my side,
And the silver pistol
You keep waving
In my face.

I'm getting somewhat
Tired of your aggression,
And tired of you
In this place.

Every choice I've
Made was not about
You or your particular disgrace.

Once walking the center line
I had to be pushed
Off that road,
onto a path that was paved.

Then I found you standing
In my way.
Go on and fire off
A round.

Let's just see
The direction that
Bullet takes.
I'd be willing to bet,
It will make more sense
Then you have ever made.

So get off my island,
Get back in your cage.
You pathetic excuse
For a human.

Go tell your stories
To someone that might
Believe the shit you say.

You're so over,
I'm so done,
With your deception,
Lies, and dramatic ways.

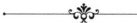

Over the years of abuse, the madness just built up. When she got all she could get from me, she finally walked out. There I was left with a lifetime's worth of tears, regret, and confusion, not to mention an empty house and a pile of bills. As she delighted in watching me fall apart, the mess she left behind was all my responsibility; I was the only one at fault. All the time, I demonstrated respect for our relationship, never saying a negative word about her, not talking trash about her to our children. I didn't think that was appropriate, and I foolishly felt she would show me the same respect.

Now, I know this was not the case. Unbeknownst to me, she was bad-mouthing me throughout our entire relationship, always devaluing and discrediting me, especially to our children. She enjoyed my begging for approval and delighted herself in my mental confusion. She exposed my darkest secrets to others. Not only that, but she was at her best when I was unhappiest, making up so many lies and incredible stories, it is no wonder my oldest daughter didn't speak to me for many years. I've learned also that she presented many dramatic scenes to my daughter and others, saying with crocodile tears, she feared I had somehow given her AIDS; apparently, I gave her some type of sexually transmitted disease also. I don't know how that could be when I didn't know about such a thing. Also, she told my daughters and who knows who else that I had relations with nineteen people during our marriage. I truly would be hard-pressed to come up with half that amount in my entire life. And that includes her. The bulk of my relationships were after she walked out on me. Really, I should have gotten some type of reward for being as committed to that marriage as much as I was. These things are so horrible and, at the same time, to absorb. I have difficulty understanding where it all came from and how anyone could make up such lies.

To others outside our home, she presented herself as a kind, sensitive, pleasant individual, always smiling and caring, except when playing the victim. Oh yes, that victim role she perfected by putting it into practice often. Her abuse was so insidious and overtly dishonest, it was truly disgusting.

Why, yes why, is another question I still have. Why did she have to destroy my relationship with my daughters? Now, my youngest daughter, whom I thought I could trust, did nothing to help me, even when I needed help the most. Somehow, all my difficulty with depression and suicide was hardest on her. I am completely responsible for putting her through hell as told by her. To this day, she regards me as someone not worthy of basic kindness or any amount of respect. She has taken herself completely out of my life, not allowing me to ever see my grandson. I know that I mean less than nothing to her and there is nothing I can do ... She has become a prodigy of her mother, a complete and total narcissist. She has never had any regard for what I was going through; it just does not matter to her.

Finally, I came to realize that nothing I could do or say would change things between my daughter and me. When I finally evaluated my situation, I got a part-time job after so many years of not being able to hold one; foolishly, I thought she would be happy for me. When telling her how good everything was going for me, she lashed out. I didn't understand what was happening at the time, and I asked her why she reacted the way she did. I explained how I'm not her enemy, not understanding why she took everything I said against her. When not even speaking about her, just like her mother, she twisted everything to be about and against her. Now, I know this is a textbook narcissist trait.

Since narcissism is a learned behavior, I thought she would at the very least realize the pattern. From her grandmother to her mother and her aunt, all of them are narcissist. They seem to feed on one another. Even though their relationships between each other are often strained at best, no one can ever break into the circle. They bad-mouth each other with very little trust, if any, between them. Yet, no one could ever even hint to saying a negative thing to one about the other. Everything is highly dramatized, each contention exposed and realized. Yet, God forbid anyone ever try and explain how there is no logic in their actions.

I'm so thankful that I have my daughter, Christine. She is the one that educated herself first. She stood up and told everyone she had had enough and would not take it anymore. I was a little slower to react, not wanting to end my relationship with Erin. No matter how unrealistic it was, she is still my daughter and my love for her is truly unconditional. If she were to ever call or show up at my door, I would still welcome her with open arms. I don't and can't harbor hate for anyone. I'm just trying to get through what is left of my life. I've found a little happiness, something I've never had, but I have faith that it does exist. My best chance looks like, if I keep loving, keep respecting, and pay close attention to Christine and start loving and respecting myself in the process, I will find that happiness and my life will be complete. Maybe, just maybe, before I pass, I might actually experience the warmth of a smile and a true loving embrace. To this late date, since I'm too old for an early grave, time is just running out. So, what's up with that?

Right now, I feel there is a future for me, and I will keep examining, educating myself, and writing, fully developing my creativity. Maybe behind my tear-stained eyes, within the aging lines that cut through my face, there might someday be a little crack, perhaps a smile. We'll see!

I have finally found a church, a community of believers that I feel are just right for me, and I've been getting involved as much as I can. Attending weekly service and Bible study is working well for me. It is a Baptist church with a large congregation, very active in the work of Christ. Recently, I was baptized and I feel great about that. My friend and spiritual guide, Dr. Jeffery Haugh, introduced me to this church, and I pray every day for his continued guidance. It will embarrass him to hear me call him a spiritual guide, but that is what he has become. He encourages me to read Scripture daily and often pray, recognizing God in everything. He is a good friend and I have grown to love and appreciate his insights.

The church community is something I've needed and searched for a long time. It is a great blessing to have that in my life; meeting new people and collecting a new set of friends is absolutely fabulous. I look forward to getting more involved as time goes on. Looking at others with a new set of eyes has added a brighter chapter in my life. No longer do I feel alone or lost, for I found a place where I belong.

I still suffer from the effects of bipolar disorder, with extreme manic and depressive episodes. It is a matter of management and how to handle these things. I don't always have triggers, so I'm never certain where it comes from; yet, I do know what will happen if I don't take action to fight off the depression. Utilizing tools such as meditation, exercising, and breathing all help. The most help I get is by reading Scripture in the morning and night. I pray for relief, and relief comes. I talk with friends in my Christian fellowship, which helps immensely. Writing and praying is the best help of all.

A Collection of Logic

A hemorrhage of thoughts and ideas,
Out of the mind,
Down through the spine
Out of a limb, then through a pen
Words are found releasing the pain
Once in the brain.

Take advantage of this,
Continue more than just being.
Setting oneself free from lies
And deceptions seen,
With eyes that no longer bleed.

So shed no more tears
Go without fear.
Orbiting around your hometown,
Stand up tall,
Try never to fall.
Tripping along each narrow path,
Although not paved
You still will be saved.

Keep chipping away
Say all you can say.
You are not yet ready
For a final epilogue.

Here, hold steady,
Get ready for the new dawn.
Never give in, but give all you have.
Make and keep friends
By being the best you can.

Never stay in a bad place,
Where they don't care how you are.
Keep moving along,
For standing too still
Will kill you before a new life begins.

It's a wonder, you know,
Those furthest away,
Are the very best and closest to your heart.

As a writer does write, a poet
Tries to bend and shape every word.
This is all just one day,
We know tomorrow will never come.

But don't fade away
All those dark corners,
Are revealed and exposed.
Light will always find
Its way in.

With all you have learned
Now you must know
You can put your trust in God;
However, remain cautious of man.

The original title of this book was *A Lone Skater on A Frozen Pond: An Exploration of Images and Ideas from a Psychotic Mind.* I had to change it after joining Maryland's Writer's Association. I was discriminated against by that group since I am a white male. At a conference, I was told, "No one would like to hear about the troubles of a white male," "You are not diverse enough," etc. I paid to give a pitch for my book, and without reading a word I've written, the woman editor said my story has no ark and that no one would be interested.

Somewhat discouraged, I left that conference feeling defeated. When I got home, I took a long look in the mirror. Not able to accept what I was being told, I changed the title to *A Survivor's Ark.* Now, tell me my story has no ark. Going from a living hell, the pit of despair, to the loving arms of Christ is all the ark I need. I cannot allow anyone to tell me my story is not interesting or that I'm somehow not valid. Now that I understand I am a child of God, that is all the encouragement I need.

Woe

Woe to my left,
Woe to my right,
Help me stay straight
On the path of Your light.

Woe to my left,
Woe to my right,
Steady my stumbles,
Balance and enlighten my mind.

Woe to my left,
Woe to my right,
I rejoice in this suffering
As it glorifies You on high.

Woe to my left,
Woe to my right,
Carry me through darkness
Until the end of all nights.

Woe, woe to left to right,
Tether my soul to
The mighty loving arms of Christ.

Morning Is Coming

Morning is coming
I rise up knowing,
He is risen, so it's a
Hallelujah day again today.

Mornings are so beautiful,
Even before the first light's ray.
For it's more than just a feeling,
Knowing that another chance is on the way.

Each calming moment is a gift of peace,
Understanding the Lord's here with
Such an undeserving one as me,
Extending hope with my belief.

So I pray every morning as I first wake.
Pray to stay on this path, His hands guided me.
Pray for my understanding and acceptance.
Pray for serenity in surrendering all worries.

My mind becomes settled with His strength,
By these gifts, returning all my offerings.
His greatness is here in yet another
Hallelujah day!

My Irish

My Irish
So I will not speak in tongues
Foreign to anyone.
Will not be caught just babbling,
For this reason, I've learned enunciation.
So listen to the sounds made
As I heavily breathe vibrating cords
In my throat forcing air to
Round out the curves of my tongue.

Speaking today I bend, and shape
The very meaning of my words.
In the singularity of this voice,
Discovering just how many ways
And times can I describe
For you, my love!

In stillness, I must say,
Every war that ever was,
Lost before it had begun.

Spilling out thoughts, I try, for
In my head are ancient Irish rovers;
Troubadours, poets, and priests announcing themselves,
With the sounds of brass trumpets and drums.

You might describe them as structureless
Or even off beat, yet it's all melodies
Clear music to me.

Still traveling through caverns
Of my soul, entering this mind

Through the eyes of my conscious desires.
All I ever asked was to be remembered,
And even heard.

Once then and now
They all were and are simply the purity
of God's Love …
Echoes of the Irish and all the
Torture surrounding so many innocents,
Graceful souls, carries a weight so heavy,
My tears must continue to flow.

A knowing of these things and those
Shadows so desperate in their needs
Keeps me breathing out with a voice
For breaking through all walls.

A Ripple

As for the Ripple in the Dead Calm
Which caused the tsunami,
I brave each wave at the shores tide
It rips my humanity by tossing me
With a pounding of unstoppable cadence
I splattered against the white sands
It takes all my strength and I know
I am wrong, for out there is
A Ripple in the Dead Calm
That caused the tsunami
On board an iron ship, a city on the forgotten sea.

Crossing channels in night storms relentlessly
We cut through the barriers of those waves,
Yet it's a Ripple in the Dead Calm
That caused the tsunami.

We are no challenge for the sea,
We were no challenge for
A ripple, on our city, on an overlooked sea,
So what started that Ripple in the Dead Calm
That caused the tsunami
Was it you, them, or me?

Total Transformation

Total transformation,
From a life of temporal affections,
Now grasping spiritual wisdom,
With eternal expectations on
A path of friendly, godly relations.

Total transformation;
Now understanding a child of God,
Now understanding the glory of Jesus,
Now understanding spiritual connection,
Now understanding this transformation,
Now understanding being poor in spirit by regulation.

So ready for public purification
by the sacrament of baptism,
The initiation of Christ relations,
Identifying with resurrection,
From the waters of death to
All the grace of God by the Glory of Jesus!

Sweetest Sound?

There is a song never heard,
It's the song of the smallest bird.
As it flies, it cries in dark solitude,
Tries and tries to find a way home.
It has no flock, it's all alone.
That song could be so beautiful,
No one will ever know,
For that bird remains alone.
Still flying, searching for safety,
A place to land, perhaps make itself
A welcome home?
That song of the smallest bird
Might just be the sweetest sound
never heard?

The Lake

The lake water is lapping low and
Slow around my feet
The east wall of the sky holds brightness
Of this mid-morning's heat
I fall back in slumber for last night again
I did not sleep.

The crickets are silent and the skeeters retreat
Into this scene where I feel complete.

There is nothing I've got that
Can be called sweet.
Fire is in my brain for the stories I keep,
Still a miracle stands here before you,
as alive, I must still be
A fractured Pause of the ebb and flow,
As cool water swirls around stones under my toes.

I'm back in a dream with you all for a quiet moment of peace.
The water lapping caresses me
Back into this perfection of glorious sleep

In Peace

As my anger subsides
Into the grace of God's Love.
My heart is full and overflows
With emotions of peaceful dynamic
Insightful, civil tones of gratitude.

I set my sight on restful love of
My enemies, my foes once out of focus,
Due to tears of rage. Calmly,
Now I see them as God's children.

A Peacemaker came to us all,
To follow Him is a want of true love.
So I follow Him to the mansion
Beyond the high of any mountain
I've ever known.

And I Pray

The majestic presence of You
Surrounds me this day;
In all Your beautiful offerings
On this Crystal Lake.

In my heart, I'm with You
As Sunshine comes my way.
I am a child that lets the
Dew clouds unfold his dreams.
I climbed the tallest trees to better see.

A river rocked my soul, I let a little scream,
Softly with excitement of outlandish glee.
The color of Your eyes I saw as
Fiery bright blue-green.

While wrapping Your loving arms around me
You infused meaning in my mind,
Harmony in my heart.
To my death
I will forever hold these glowing dreams.

What will never pass is Your love, I see.
No daylight will ever make You fade away.
You brought me to this foundation,
Now I will never leave.

And I ache with a renegade
Of desire flanked by my mistakes,
Immorality, impurity, enmity,
Such strife of drunken envy,
Earthly evil, covetous wants.

I die aching in unholy captivity,
Anger rivals dissensions
Of my heart; heavy from sorrow,
I pull away to end a day
Trouble in this tide, I die by the breakers
To swim no more treads my heart, my soul,
Wanting to hold another, but loneliness takes over.

In this stillness I lay and ache a life away.
Oh, Merciful God, awake for
I am ready for Thou to take

Cried for Love

The wing of an angel,
The sound of the dove,
Oppression set the tone,
For depression to come along.

Alone in the chamber of isolation,
Breaking chains that bruise the bone,
I fall down in a lonely room,
Again, with the groans and moans.

Within the walls of insanity,
I come in waiting to comfort
My soul's profound destiny.
The fight begins the night's wane
Again and again on this dark earth.

By dawn, I believe in His mercies
With all my mistakes washed away by the rain,
So please let it rain again and again.

A Man of God (revisited)

Met that day a stranger kind,
An honest man now a friend of mine;
We sat a spell in lots of time
A working man, so sublime.

Extending outward, a helping hand,
His selfless offerings in peaceful sighs;
Eternal wonderment at his command,
Better than the best of man.

He offers up simple prayers,
From deep within his heart, soul, and mind;
A mentor of life's purposeful sway,
This gentleman passions plea,
Defining the true spirit, a man can be.

Angels surround him to take someday,
My prayers all answered for this delay;
Each moment of time are gifts God gave
A righteous man, a wise sage.

As God will never betray,
In my heart, this man of God
Will forever stay.

Oh, Lord!

Let me praise thee in each poetic stave, find you in major ways. A glance, a romance, a dance, hold true Your trust in me.

I beg, I plead, I pray this day feeling now as one unscathed. Announce Yourself surrounding me, help me cherish my life, abide within me, advance my will for integrity. Allow me to serve Thee in ways not yet known to me. Forgive me, have mercy, know me, advise me. Allow me to walk beside Thee, with these many gifts You give abundantly; may I use them sparingly to flush out my unworthiness. Set before me Your holy net. I cherish these gifts; please take all my meager offerings. release my fear, let me feed the spirit within me.

I pray on my knees before thee!

This Day's Longing

As the wind blows
Hard against these
Mountains,
My eyes are leveled,
Setting sight over the sea.

My soul captures
Emotions foreign and
Brightly new to me.

A true gift of unfathomable
Dimensions stands so
Close I crumble at her
Inter-terrestrial intelligence.

This blood from my very being,
A circle of life surrounding,
Enveloping love over everything.

Each step, breath, and move
My old man's body allows me
To take are my offerings.

Keeping pace today, yet
Tomorrow I'll have to go away.

I go a better man, fulfilled,
With truth and sense of true father
And how it is the very best of who
I am.

Reverent Reminder

My Creator, the omnipotent,
Above all there is or ever was,
Holding true dominion over all,
Yesterday, today, and beyond.

He taught me to speak, not what to say;
Gives me abundant gifts of
Blessings, sign's strength,
Willful might in mindful ways.

Helps me walk upright and free,
Reminds me my ancestors paid
With blood, stood in bondage, held as slaves.

My Creator gives me purpose as
An empathic seer who feels love,
As well as the world's suffering
From man's worldly ways.

He accepts me as I am, now a faithful man
No one can impute or stand against,
The man I've become today.

He loves us in equal amounts,
Yet we are different but the same;
My Creator allows me to fill these
Blank pages as they hold my
Soulful, thankful, grateful staves.

It is to my Creator I pray!

Hope

A rush of silence, broken with
The hint of a forbidden kiss.
Dreams in stillness, lucid with brightness.

So glad those sad eyes did not miss.
A heart in love is still a gift
If meant to be, they'll be a key.

In waves of passion, a song explicit
Tempered with melodies, softness.
Voices of change are without regret.

Receive and hold the very best;
Destiny is pure in love's fortress.
Bearing fruit dispels all myths.

Faith Walk

I wake before first light,
My routine, deliberate and safe.
Your presence is strong and everlasting,
As the essence of life comes through
The darkest crevice of time.

My anticipation is heavily steeped in belief
When I walk toward Your grace.
A wavelength of might insights the love You give.

Your affection; my gratitude is steadfast,
With abundance on this path with your light.
I go to the valley without a shadow of doubt;
My walk with You is that of complete faith.

Dawn

My work boots remain empty,
At the foot of the bed,
Curtains closed, light is limited and still.

My room is in obscure shadows;
Staying in this day's long-suffering,
No sound mocking a new dawn.

Nothing licit or familiar of wakefulness,
Insensitive clocks scream out time to rise up;
A dull beating heart has stopped
The unique succession of youthful banter,
Now a lasting horror spawned to its death,
And I am no longer home.

To Trip

I trip, I stumble,
Out of time, I fall,
So thankful
For my unfailing Guide.

Weakness carries much grief,
He guides me out of my unbelief.

False impressions, entangled memories,
He takes me to right solutions with clarity.

My mind expresses doubt
With shame and guilt;
He takes my hand and guides me
Into light,
With a greater understanding
Of truth, not doubt.

With diseased perceptions, failed expectation,
Promises made, I often forget.
From appearance of sickness
Into wholeness of health.

Once filled with fear, self-recrimination, and blame,
He guided me out of my sense of lack
Into abundant provisions with goodness in kindness.

In a lapse of reason, I lost my mind.
In my hours of need, He is always there,
My unfailing Guide.

Forty Days

Forty days without you,
So long without a word,
On this starlit beach,
Tracing your footsteps.

Under the weight of the waves,
I've lost what I've traced,
Your impressions of such grace,
Empty on this endless beach.

This mad-man's paradise,
With each sunset, sand turns
To pebbles than rocks as time
Turns away from me.

Forty days and my feet bleed,
A burning image with unanswered
Question as to what did change.

Lost impressions and my blood,
Rushing out to sea,
A mentor once in love,
Now what does remain,
But more dark endings
Of the forty days.

My Door

My door solid sturdy unopened in
Years once measured out in weeks,
Hinges rusted by now surely creek,
The failing lock housing spiders
With flies that made a mistake.

My pale flaking flesh softened,
Making many meals for worms' relief.

My soul has gone beyond these
Walls that still can't speak.

I melt in this chair, forgotten,
For no one provided a eulogy.

The air is still and moist,
Thick with ammonia that drives
A cadence down the hall of lost memories.

A life in loneliness
Is all they have to say.

Raw courage it took to last
As long as I did, anyway.

Walk with God

Walk in the Spirit,
Read the Word,
Relate to Jesus.

Take in the answers,
Fulfill your mission,
Breathe beyond your will.

Learn to know thyself,
Rise above suffering
With wings of the dove.

Consciously reach for God's
Everlasting love;
Always look up to His love,
Always give into that love,
Always be in touch with His love,
Settle into a life of divine intervention,
As you walk with God.

Interpret This

A lucid, intense vision in a dream,
I was paralyzed by its sight;
A burning screaming bleeding piece of wood.
Felt once it had been well planned, and small.
Now growing larger, getting closer;
Then felt the extreme heat,
I could hear the high-pitched screams,
Smell the burning blood.

Clearly see the multidimensional grains
It must have taken years to grow.
Vivid colors, deep texture before me;
A burning screaming bleeding piece of wood.

Floating in midair with nothingness all around,
A knowing of truth, intensely felt,
For if I stay my path, that would be my end;
The only answer was to change
And find a different path,
One of righteousness,
To the eternal Dream of peace.

This cup before me is empty
Trying to remember, did I drink?
Can I ask for another on the road
Or the path laid out in front of me.

The songs of summer long gone
Stifle pursuit of a warm breeze,
Futile white flowers given her
Representing love's eternal dream.

In humble worship, worries diminished,
An open door leads to a path, narrow and steep;
Sleep escapes dawn's mysteries that
Nobody wants or sees.

Darkness relates more than hours of night,
For it can black out a high noon sunny day;
It's not sight, it's a feeling of stillness which
meditates all the love God gave.

Overhead, a fan circulates the room's emptiness,
As I contemplate inside me, the very same;
Nothing is new here, nothing to see but
A fool wasting an hour, a day, a life thinking in staves.

A blink of the eye surely is all it takes
To see the truest love ever was or will be,
Something about the twinkling stars,
A night sky fading out to gray.

On the day I was born,
Legions laid down their arms,
Leaving me to fight this battle on my own,
The strength I receive is all the Lord gave.

Water rises from my tears,
Still wouldn't have it any other way.

Bless this day!

My God, My God, My Sweet Lord!

I'm counting on Your divine intervention,
Send me a word, send me
Something for my situation, my salvation.

You've unlocked Heaven's door;
Although the path is narrow and thin,
The invitation is the same for every man.

I put a candle in my window,
I'll put a cross on my door,
I'll do whatever You ask, Lord.

Walking in the dusk of time,
Once, I went by way of a hard line;
Oh! did I pray to show me this new way

You've taken my burdens away,
Smiles fall on me abundantly, silently;
You softened my heart, touch my soul,
Hold me in Your arms, envelop me
With Your unlimited love.

Keep teaching me Your way,
My God, My God, My sweet Lord!

My Brother

My brother,
Be of good cheer.

There are no aerial boundaries,
His spirit is endless,
Surrounding us throughout,
Our counsel of years.

Your wholesome goodness remains,
When disciplining the mind's thoughts.
Filtered by the heart's desires to be pure.

Not to distress, for God's love is to all,
Never wanted our feigned affections.
Labor no confusion for
Our Lord and Savior,
He is forever here!

Scarf of Pale Blue,

Blue silk on hair of scarlet,
Her beauty fogged my spectacles.

What is there for me to do?
A thin strip of black velvet wrapped,
Such graceful grace on grace,
The sweetness of her voice,
Held captured in her everlasting smile.

Those long dark eyelashes,
The wind, for luck, has stolen a few.

When will love, for me, be true?
I remember that scarf of pale blue.

No scent man has ever made,
Could challenge her truth.

Spending my life watching others,
That do enjoy the gifts of love.

I was witness to the fallen stars;
Still, my arms remain empty,
Just what is it about,
That scarf of pale blue?

Can't cross the river

For it's too deep and wide.
I've got to believe and hold
The hand of God as though
I'm a child trying to survive.
All the steps I've taken brought
Me here by His side.
The light shines and glistens off
The water and tears in His eyes.
I remember the beginning
How all the love felt so right.
Now I need to see Him
I need Him in my life.
This world is not my home,
So I desire to walk with Jesus
To restore what was lost in Paradise.
I'm building on the strength of a dream
The one I had last night.

In this stay

With these words that,
I shamelessly steal from,
Strangers that obviously,
allowed themselves to dream.

 I fall back into the sty
of that darkest driven beast.
The entity which gave to me,
a stark contrast between lights of gray, by
each lesson in realities that bleed more than me.

There is a dream that tried to escape
passing by this lowly soldier who,
never was a child with a mother.
Now wrapped up in grips of love.
Now freed to be that child of God.

With these wounds of agony,
wounds of grief,
wounds of confusion,
wounds that dared me to speak,
comes strengths from that spirit of God.

A sense of purpose is here today.
All my burdens have found relief.
Showered in joyous gifts
of purest love offerings.
In moments, I split, I found a way to sleep.

So here is my falling leafs, as my time,
turns with this season's change.
Somewhere there is a wreck that remains.
But I'm walking on a pure white beach,
with the sweetest air, I can finally breathe.

Kevin J Ryan

Printed in the USA
CPSIA information can be obtained
at www.ICGtesting.com
LVHW040350290224
772928LV00003B/431